A LITERARY AFFAIR

A LITERARY AFFAIR

MARIE-CLAIRE BLAIS

Translated by Sheila Fischman

McCLELLAND AND STEWART

**NORTHWEST COMMUNITY
COLLEGE**

Originally published as *Une Liaison Parisienne,* copyright
©1975 by Les Ecrivains Coopératif d'Edition.

This translation, *A Literary Affair,* translated by Sheila
Fischman, copyright©1979 by McClelland and Stewart
Limited

The Canadian Publishers
McClelland and Stewart Limited
25 Hollinger Road
Toronto M4B 3G2

CANADIAN CATALOGUING IN PUBLICATION DATA

Blais, Marie-Claire, 1939-
  [Une liaison parisienne. English]
  A Literary Affair

Translation of Une liaison parisienne.

ISBN 0-7710-1559-3
I. Title. II. Title: Une liaison parisienne.
English.

PS8503.L35L513 C843'.5'4 C79-094256-9
PQ3919.2.B53L513

The content and characters in this book are fiction.
Any resemblance to actual persons or happenings
is coincidental.

This translation was completed with the support
of The Canada Council.

Printed and bound in Canada
by John Deyell Company

To Guy Delavier
M-C B.

For David Homel
S.F.

"All that, I fancied, I had imagined, and as it turned out the world was quite different; all was so joyful for me, and so comfortable; I still had . . . but forget that. Alas, all was done in the name of love, the grandeur of the soul, honour, and subsequently everything became monstrous, insolent, discreditable."

Dostoyevsky

I

When Mathieu Lelièvre, author of a first novel soon to be published in Paris, armed with a Canada Council grant that made him already rich in his own imagination, boarded the plane for Paris in Montreal that year, how impatient he was to see the land he had revered since childhood – France, Paris! For he was on his way not only to a reconciliation with the Europe of his ancestors, close now at last to his modern and romantic heart – a reconciliation with the underground Quebec whose rumblings of rebellion he took with him everywhere – but, as he had announced to his poet friends at the airport, he was finally on his way to Life. At the word Life he would sigh, not daring to add anything more for fear of breaking the spell of his hopes, the hopes of a twenty-year-old boy whom the practice of misfortune, experience, had scarcely bruised or startled, had scarcely cut into. Perhaps this was so because Mathieu Lelièvre had learned early, from his mother, that "even if you're born lucky you should rise above your fate" or else because he had been born that way, the product of another time and another world, naïve and virginal in heart and mind. One morning, then, he set off for grey Europe, sole member of his uncommon species, it might have been said. It is true that no one wished to be like him, not even in his own country; when his comrades spoke of revolution he would shamelessly protest that he liked only French literature, quoting Balzac and

Proust and denouncing the fury of weapons; and if the love of France that had always obsessed and nourished him seemed sacrilegious to his friends, Mathieu Lelièvre's indifference to any and all selective and political ideology placed him clearly among the "traitors." The only friend he still had, Pierre-Henri Lajeunesse, also enamoured of France, was one of those unreliable friends who was frank enough to say, "I'll betray you too, some day," but who, in Quebec, predict their approaching betrayal with an almost veiled delicacy by adding: "I change quickly, you see, I move with the times, I'm preparing for other metamorphoses," which left Mathieu a little time to dream. At twenty-five, Pierre-Henri Lajeunesse was "a dandy who lived by his pen" and already burnt-out; he would speak of his age to Mathieu as he smoked his pipe and nodded over "the *oeuvre* of his maturity"; but he crossed the ocean and travelled the world with a tireless ardour that made him precious to Mathieu, to whom he said: "I can introduce you to places sacred to the arts in Paris, dear friend. Yes, you'll see, it's quite a privilege for an indigent North American like you. And it couldn't be easier — you need only hand this envelope to Madame d'Argenti, a woman who is, you'll see, the quintessence of French life. So refined, so elegant! She has only one flaw — she sometimes contracts a few debts in her husband's name; but is that really a flaw?" For Pierre-Henri Lajeunesse seemed to respect that kind of snobbery in his European friends, "to seem to be a rich Canadian — something that doesn't even exist yet as a myth, you see; we speak only of the rich American, and that's how you buy love when you're nothing but a colonized Québécois!" And he would thus squander his entire inheritance, which brought him little love, but a great deal of disdain, for in Paris people said of him: "Who's that poor fool from Quebec who gives away all his money?"

Mathieu, already fascinated by the mysterious writer, asked several questions: "Have you seen her more than once? Where does she live?" Pierre-Henri boasted of having been invited to visit Madame d'Argenti on Ile Saint-Louis. "Of course," he said with an air of detachment, "I'd noticed her several times at literary cocktail parties. What a woman! Ever since, we've been writing to each other. She confides all her worries to me and I help her however I can; this envelope contains a small sum for her, poor angel – such a delicate soul! You'll see!" Pierre-Henri Lajeunesse declared straightforwardly that "a courtesan must always be lucid," and that Paris had taught him a smiling obsequiousness that might be indispensable when one wished to advance in life, "and that didn't seem to be such a bad education after all, for anything might be useful to us, bastards that we are." Mathieu listened to him absently, imagining himself already in his garret, writing night and day, leaving his nest of inspirations only to smoke a cigarette as he contemplated the beauty of Paris. The room was waiting for him when he arrived: located near the Gare d'Austerlitz, it was ugly, its anonymity only emphasizing its ugliness, and so cold and dark that Mathieu left his bags and quickly went back down to the street. As he walked he told himself that only a cold shower could deliver him from the langour of his night flight, and with his memory still haunted by the range of soaps advertised on television in his country – Lifebuoy, Safeguard, Cool – he grew sad because there were so few French sounds in these commercial appeals to cleanliness. Then he remembered that he was to telephone Madame d'Argenti, and her melodious name – Yvonne, Yvonne d'Argenti – sounded so sweet to his ear that suddenly he began to believe it was all true, that he was no longer dreaming, that he was at last in France.

For a long time he had looked for a telephone and now at last he was holding against his cheek the instrument he had not yet learned to master in his new homeland, although at home the telephone seemed to be a natural extension of one's body. No, Mathieu Lelièvre could not imagine a French Canadian who was not extended by this object,

13

which, when brought near the heart and voice, becomes superior to all others; in Paris, however, the object's inaccessibility helped him discover how intoxicating it was to hear an unknown voice, the barely audible voice of Yvonne d'Argenti murmuring, "Yes, yes, this is she." Then there was a crackling and the voice no longer reached his clouded senses. He barely had time to complete his mission – the letter from Pierre-Henri Lajeunesse – but as soon as he spoke of his friend, Madame d'Argenti's voice was firmer: "Come on Sunday," she said, "we'll be expecting you," and the sound of her crystalline voice, rather distant, however, and slightly imperious, transformed Mathieu Lelièvre, exhausted traveller, into the hero of a novel. In this chosen city he was suddenly certain that he would be able to love: perhaps he would not be loved in return, but that was of little concern, for as he had told Pierre-Henri Lajeunesse, he was "first of all a writer and therefore an observer" and this role, theoretical though it might be, required him to be constantly attentive, "rigorously analytical, and to leave behind the lover of experience." "Isn't it dangerous to choose both at once?" asked Pierre-Henri, but Mathieu replied that despite his ignorance he felt he was "a wise man surrounded by fools," and that his rational vigilance would always save him from peril. Pierre-Henri Lajeunesse smiled haughtily at his friend: "That's what happens," he said, "to those who, like you, have no imagination, who choose reason and get kicked in the pants sooner than anyone else!"

On Sunday Mathieu Lelièvre made the mistake of arriving too early for dinner at the d'Argentis. He rang the bell, and as he was standing on the doorstep, all fearful in his "trench coat" (despite his love of linguistic purity he acknowledged that he had never been able to find a French word to designate the garment), he felt rage kindling in his hosts' house, perhaps even because of him. Cats, a dog, the angry voice of a man, adolescent wailing – a considerable tempest was rumbling at the appearance of this unpolished individual who had come to disturb the delightful peace of a family alone with its Sunday and itself. But Yvonne d'Argenti was standing before him and when Mathieu Lelièvre saw her he told himself that Pierre-Henri "had not praised this woman in vain." "A charming woman," he thought, and made his way, filled with awe, beneath the shadowy vault of the small apartment. He who had always hungered for details now hoped that from this moment he would never forget the quiet shadows of late afternoons in Paris; he contemplated the rich foliage suggested by the velvet-covered walls as if to devour it with his eyes and then, gripped by the intimacy of this poetry focussed on shadow, let himself sink into the armchair he had been offered, fearing his own lethargy when he was surrounded by too much beauty. He knew that as he looked, contemplated, around him he would soon grow lazy, sensual. "Dinner will be served later," said Yvonne d'Argenti, "because of my moronic son." Mathieu Lelièvre stared at Yvonne d'Argenti with flashing eyes. "Moronic son – she can't have said that, I didn't hear her properly," Mathieu thought, unaware that Madame d'Argenti did not like to feel creeping over her, upon her crimson cheeks and along her sculptural nose, "this boy's devastating indecency," and that compared with her own refinement that boy, whom she was seeing for the first time at her home, "had the manners of a savage!" But because she was tolerant, and because Mathieu Lelièvre was perhaps "only timid, after all," she allowed him to stare to his satisfaction, and reassured her guest with a smile.

"Come," she said, "Let me introduce you to my husband."

Antoine d'Argenti was reading in the next room: he was a handsome, indolent man deep in a shadowy armchair, whom Mathieu liked immediately; perhaps he even saw in Antoine one more prince to add to his Parisian mythology, having imagined just such an elegant man at Madame d'Argenti's side. Mathieu shook his hand in a keen burst of fellow-feeling, as he would have done on meeting a friend in a

Montreal tavern, which brought from his host a surprised look and a distancing gesture that seemed to say: "See here, my young friend, let's not go too far." It was a gesture that Mathieu interpreted as a discreet, and perhaps deserved, reprimand, "for one must always place oneself in the position of those who see us from a different point of view," he thought. "A moron, yes, I assure you, an absolute moron," Madame d'Argenti repeated as saucepans rattled in the kitchen. "She's most likely angry," Mathieu thought as he listened to her heap insults on her son; "I've offended her by arriving too early," he thought again, "though Pierre-Henri told me that with the French you should always allow a good quarter of an hour." Still, it must be highly annoying for Madame d'Argenti to feel that there was in her house a witness to her rage, a rage that was perhaps infrequent, even uncharacteristic. Would it not be more appropriate to leave Pierre-Henri's envelope on the table and then discreetly flee? He was walking towards the door when Madame d'Argenti's smile suddenly disarmed him: "Come, my friend, let's have a quiet chat. Ah! the envelope, I'd forgotten . . . Thank you. Your friend is so generous and I have so many worries . . . My son is preparing dinner, he's an unhappy child but he's so witless he's unbearable . . . Don't forget to thank your friend Pierre-Henri. Ah! that young man understands everything; he knew how urgently I needed this small sum . . . " Mathieu Lelièvre watched Madame d'Argenti, regretting that he was not the one who, like Pierre-Henri Lajeunesse, "that capitalist who lives off his father's fortune and keeps telling me how he's a poor colonized Québécois," could lighten the "urgent needs" of such a kind woman, whose humility delighted him. She had merely to look his way, her grey eyes begging for a kind word, a silent compliment, and he wanted to prolong indefinitely this exchange in which nothing was happening but in which he could sense so many hopes for the morrow.

"It's simpler to serve dinner in 'Antoine's room,' " said Yvonne d'Argenti, leading Mathieu into a tiny, barely lit salon; how Mathieu prized the closed-in, smoke-darkened rooms of these old apartments – he who had always lived within the four-square walls of modern architecture! How simple it seemed to him, in these places, to pursue his inner delectation as he discovered his place in time among old things – he who saw himself as "a spirit from the past in blue jeans." The d'Argenti family, however, did not see Mathieu in the flattering light "of the past" at all: each in turn observed him with amused concentration, and nothing seemed newer or more barbaric to them than this dishevelled creature who had landed in their salon.

"Ah yes, Canada!" Madame d'Argenti sighed. "I'm so very fond of Canadians," and saying this she seemed so magnanimous that Mathieu was astonished when, a moment later, she shouted at her son who was entering the salon with the fish course:

"Have you lost your mind? What are you doing here?"

"I'm serving the fish as you told me to do," and a thin boy with an undershot jaw appeared; he was the moron Madame d'Argenti had talked about. "Put it down then, imbecile, it's obviously burning hot . . . Not on the Louis XV . . . Ah! what a fool! Not on your father's piano! Do you have any brains in your head?" Mathieu wondered why such an amusing and original creature, with his unique manner of flying over the heads of the guests with his platter of fish, had been so nicknamed; perhaps, he mused, the word "moron" in the indulgent mouth of Madame d'Argenti was simply a term of affection, a joke that praised her son's dreamy virtues.

Yet she seemed livid with rage, and she snatched the platter from his hands, adding severely: "You make a mess of everything, don't you? You'll never change."

But Paul, the son, replied softly: "What about the cats? What shall I do with them?"

"You must prepare their *faux-filet!* Come now, what are you waiting for, the poor creatures are starving!"

"There's no more *faux-filet.*"

17

"Go and buy some then, can't you hear them crying from privation? Are you so heartless you can't even think of them? The poor animals!"

Mathieu Lelièvre enjoyed this evening conversation: as Madame d'Argenti served the fish he gazed languidly at Antoine d'Argenti's luxurious collection of books; everywhere he looked in this house, in fact, he felt the sadness of memory. For he had dreamed so long of being inside these houses of the past, he had brushed so often against shadows and light because of his love of French painting, that now only a familiar atmosphere stood out against his deepest memories, like these book titles, the murmur of a family's evening conversation, and the profile of Antoine d'Argenti which he compared with the profile of Pericles. The conversation went on, however, lacklustre and subdued.

"We had a maid, but unfortunately she left us," said Madame d'Argenti. "We'll get another though. One can always find another maid, don't you think?"

"You won't if you keep treating them as you've done," said a muffled voice, and Mathieu saw a second adolescent walk out of the shadows. He was sturdier than the first and was scratching his bare torso with satisfaction. "Be quiet, you," said Madame d'Argenti; "couldn't you at least dress for dinner?"

And referring to the absence of a maid, she said to her husband: "As I told you, Antoine, whether they come from Portugal or Spain, one can always find one of those little . . . " Antoine d'Argenti seemed to acquiesce as he stroked the back of a cat that slipped quickly into the domestic scenery. "He's fifteen years old, poor beast," said Madame d'Argenti, "fifteen. He's seen a good many hardships. He certainly knows about that side of life!"

"Indeed, yes!" said Antoine, looking at his wife with compassion.

"It's really quite surprising, what a cat can know," said Madame d'Argenti.

"And such intelligence, such faithfulness, such a memory especially," her husband replied.

Mathieu, still absorbed in his reminiscences, would have liked to know whether he had ever seen before the combination of colours in Antoine d'Argenti's garments. These people practised the art of living with such subtlety, he thought, that when they put on tweed trousers and a red velvet jacket in the morning they are unaware that, without wishing to do so, they are composing a tableau; and so it was that at the end of a day, a day like so many others for them, but so exceptional for him, a Québécois found himself a note of mourning in this richly coloured tapestry.

"But you're not eating."

He looked down at his fish and had the good fortune to feel that Yvonne d'Argenti was moving closer to him on her stool, and that his appetite was returning too as he listened to her speak about religion with her husband. What culture, what mystical ardour, he thought, and what eloquence they both display! She was close to him, so palpable that his eyes could follow the curve of her white arm, finding at the end a pretty hand, rather childlike, with short fingers; the perfection of the little finger delighted him as a symbol of innocence. Madame d'Argenti told her husband, with a transcendent vibration in her voice that so touched Mathieu: "You alone understand how much I love God! Ah! what is this life we live? We know, you and I, that it is only transitory!" Happy are those who know it with such conviction, Mathieu thought, for he himself had many doubts. He didn't dare tell the d'Argentis that he venerated only one religion – art – for that would be too profane after their elevated conversation. "You love life just as passionately," Antoine d'Argenti said to his wife. "Passionately, yes; only you know me so well, Antoine," she replied, clasping her hands; then addressing her son, she said in another tone:

"Why are you making so much noise?"

"I'm clearing the table and cleaning up, just as you told me to do," said Paul.

"He's so incompetent!"

Meanwhile, Antoine d'Argenti was praising for Mathieu

19

the "classical rigour" of his wife's novels, "the complexity of her analyses," and Mathieu listened, overwhelmed.

"You'll see, Mathieu, Yvonne is an exalting person, she'll never cease to astonish you."

Mathieu Lelièvre tried to gather to the depths of his being, for his store of "future memories," the warmly enveloping atmosphere that surrounded them all – people, furniture, cats – when the telephone rang, alarming the entire family, suddenly shattering its pictorial spell. Antoine d'Argenti changed positions to light a cigarette.

"Answer it, idiot!" said Yvonne d'Argenti to her son Christian, who was leaning insolently against the mantlepiece.

"What shall I say? Are you here or not?"

"You know very well I'm not. This boy is retarded, too!"

She dashed towards the telephone in the vestibule, and Mathieu was moved once more to hear "the telephone voice" that belonged only to her, he thought, the timid voice that sounded like a plea, and showed Mathieu how "fragile" the woman was.

"Yes, Madame de Cordeboix, we'll be there, yes, at five o'-clock. How kind you are! How good of you! Is Monsieur well? He's better now? My poor dear friend! You were very concerned. I know . . . Until then, dear friend."

When she came back into the salon Mathieu noticed that her cheeks were burning, at least he felt that Madame d'Argenti's cheeks became redder and more fiery, arousing in him again the instinct to protect "the fragile person" he had just discovered. How he liked her when she was this way! Madame d'Argenti, however, seemed suddenly to forget Mathieu's presence, as she spoke stiffly to her husband:

"Those tiresome Cordeboix again, inviting us for Thursday. Have you ever seen a more dreadful woman, with all her jewels and such a ridiculous husband? You'll come, Antoine, I hope, they have some superb property in Tunisia, that compensates for their ridiculous side to some extent, and they often invite famous artists, which is always important for me. Answer me, Antoine, will you come?"

"Perhaps," Antoine replied wearily.

Mathieu Lelièvre was thinking only of Madame d'Argenti's cheeks. The wine soothed the pounding of his heart. "But I must have a handbag for that evening, Antoine." "I can't give you another one this time, my dear." "What do you mean, can't? It's a tiny little bag, nothing at all . . . Practically nothing . . . two hundred francs. What's two hundred francs to you?" "I assure you, my dear, I cannot." Mathieu was astonished that a man apparently so docile could be so unrelenting towards his wife. "No," he repeated, "we won't speak of it again." Antoine's refusal seemed completely unfair. How could this understanding husband steal from the one he loved the pittance for a handbag? Such economy disgusted him. Madame d'Argenti, affected by her husband's attitude, came and sat close to Mathieu and a sullen expression darkened her face. Suddenly she took Mathieu's hands in hers and said in an aggrieved tone: "Ah! your friend Pierre-Henri Lajeunesse is so generous. One day the boy and I were walking along the Faubourg Saint-Honoré and I saw something exquisite, a cape for rainy days, in a window. I said to your friend: 'Ah, how pretty that is!' and you won't believe me, but one must be a Québécois to act as he did, for it's something one rarely sees here. What did your friend do? Guess! He went into the shop and came out with the cape. It was useless to protest, the gift was too magical and I believe in magic – don't I, Antoine?" Antoine nodded agreement. "I accepted, what else could I do under the circumstances; one can only pay tribute to a person's kindness, yes, believe me, your friend Pierre-Henri Lajeunesse has a noble soul!"

Mathieu Lelièvre would have liked to rid himself forever of the spectre of his friend; for was it not a great misfortune to be born not only with no inheritance, but with no hope of some day coming into one? No, he would not become a vile lover of the "buck," like Pierre-Henri; he would seduce Madame d'Argenti with his mind; the body would come later, if the mind failed. Had she not noticed how intuitive he was, how precocious – not that he was ahead of his century, but because he was behind the times, for originality today consisted of deliberately putting off foolishness. It's true that his poems had been savaged by the critics, but his first novel wouldn't be; published in France, land of intelligence, Mathieu Lelièvre thought, he would finally be appreciated, and Pierre-Henri, the materialist, would be jealous. Mathieu left that evening bearing signed copies of the works of Madame d'Argenti, the cautious approval of her husband, and the promise to see them all again soon. As soon as he was back in his room he read, in a state of fatigue bordering on intoxication, the books of the woman he already called his "friend." In a novel called *La Troisième Personne* Mathieu learned that Madame d'Argenti found "the number three" deeply repugnant for, as she wrote, "in life it is possible to live only in twos," which seemed sound to Mathieu. Did he not feel the same disgust when he discovered, at the beginning of his affair with a delightful woman, the spectre of his best friend? He also learned that Madame d'Argenti did not like children, especially her own, and he approved of that too, for any honest confession such as "Be careful, I'm nasty, I'm cowardly, watch out for me, I could even be criminal . . . " promptly drew absolution from him, so that after lavishing forgiveness on the contrite heart of Madame d'Argenti, he descended with delight into her style, admiring the stroke of her pen which was both ravishing and perfidious, and fell asleep attempting to solve the mystery surrounding the murder of a child in a ravine. Yvonne d'Argenti came to him in a dream, holding out her arms from the depth of a stormy landscape as she said: "Come, I am so lonely," and he awoke, savouring the final sensation of his dream; he had tasted Madame d'Argenti's tears, and the freshness of her fine temples, so he knew that henceforth she would be less lonely. Why should he not offer her the accessory she needed for Thursday evening? Happily for Mathieu, Madame d'Argenti had given her husband the information necessary to purchase the gift – the name of the shop, the street number. All that was missing now was the appearance of the "magic gift" itself. *Mon Dieu,* the people on the other side of the ocean are earthbound, he thought; could one imagine a woman speaking to her husband of "a gift with magical powers" when she coveted a fur coat?

No, Mathieu's mother would simply tell her husband: "I saw a nice fur coat at Simpsons," and for this woman with her authoritarian good sense there would be no question, as there was for Madame d'Argenti of "a humble request" but rather of "an insinuation." For the d'Argentis, though, the word "magic" was a link in an ancestral chain of fine points and poetic tricks.

Once Mathieu Lelièvre was inside the shop he was besieged by saleswomen who were nervous and exasperated even though it was still early in the morning; he told himself that although they might look like prison guards, it was because they felt misunderstood, if one were to judge by the swarm of customers pestering them without respite. Perhaps, too, they felt they were somewhat looked down on by the caste they had to serve – or were they looking down on Mathieu Lelièvre because he himself was not a member of that caste? Mathieu's ambition was "to understand all the French people," to wend his way among all the ranks of society, to drink in every café in Paris – but this morning, he felt, his fraternal hope seemed laughable.

"What do you want, Monsieur? This handbag? It's five hundred francs, Monsieur."

"No, two hundred, I was told it was only two hundred."

"I know my business better than you do."

"Well, I'll soon have my royalties," Mathieu thought, "why hesitate over three hundred francs? Would Madame d'Argenti?"

He understood as he paid the saleswoman, who had become suddenly quite friendly, that his hesitation had been perceived as impolite. One must not hesitate in this city, for reticence indicated slow-wittedness.

"Are you from Quebec, Monsieur?"

"Yes," he said proudly.

"You don't have even a trace of that slight Québecois accent," said the saleswoman.

The young perfumed woman gave him his package, leaving him to muse on her tactful words. He liked Paris more and more.

The following Wednesday he rang the d'Argentis' doorbell for the second time; he was holding his gift and Madame d'Argenti said when she saw him on the doorstep:

"In Paris, one telephones before coming to visit . . . Besides, I was washing my hair, you really are disturbing me, but come in, I need someone to open the oysters . . . Come . . ." Her voice already sounded more conciliatory. One might even have said that the sweetness of pleasure was illuminating her face, which was still wet under her hair, its curls streaming onto her shoulders, and that in spite of everything this pleasure was related to the surprise caused by Mathieu Lelièvre holding a beribboned object in his fingertips. He strongly suspected that she must be thinking: "He doesn't know how to behave in society," but if she were also thinking: "I'll teach him" all would be saved. As he was opening the oysters he thought, what intimacy: here he was opening oysters in Madame d'Argenti's kitchen, and this evidence of culinary confidence seemed to him a sign of an authentic and truly French hospitality; he was moved as he contemplated the empty apartment, and comforted at the thought that they would eat lunch alone, like old friends; and this shared ease in the middle of the day incited him to affection. He was still vaguely troubled, though, by "a stifling atmosphere" in Madame d'Argenti's books that he had read the night before, but perhaps he had read them too negligently . . . For he was, after all, a novice compared with this accomplished artist. The impression that still drifted through his mind was of a couple frantically seeking happiness; for love, as Madame d'Argenti said in her books, was a struggle, often a desperate one, between two people hungry for the same satisfactions, and at times such struggles demanded sacrifices; in this hunt, moreover, the prey was often innocent. A happy couple, their twelve-year-old son, a trip to Greece during which the son disappeared . . . But the novelist's art is such a fine one that Mathieu Lelièvre let himself be so carried away by the lyrical reality described in Madame d'Argenti's novels that he entered a sort of life that was even more transformed than the other, and he reproached real life for its lies, as he recognized in Madame d'Argenti's dreamed incarnations fragments of pure reality. At the end of one of her books the author, in the guise of one of her characters, had written: "My voice comes from another world, from a place without awareness, from a land deaf to any appeal for pity," and this statement stirred Mathieu to the depths of his soul; he told himself that it possessed a tone of confidence that transformed an ordinary reader like him into a solemn participant in the human ceremony, where writer and reader together spring, with a single voice, from this "land deaf to any appeal for pity" — even if the meaning of the phrase remained obscure to him.

"Come now, wipe your hands on this cloth," said Yvonne d'Argenti as she went into the kitchen, drying her hair, "and come into Antoine's room with me."

In the sunny light of noon, Antoine's room bore no resemblance to the shadowy retreat Mathieu had encountered on his Sunday visit; it was now only a man's room where one takes by surprise, in the still warm disorder of articles of clothing left on the chairs and the untidiness of a bed abandoned in haste, the secrets of the night. "A valet, yes, we need a valet for Antoine," said Madame d'Argenti, suddenly bitter, as she put away her husband's clothes and covered the sofa with its crimson coverlet, raising a cloud of dust that fell onto Mathieu's head. "Antoine cannot live without servants, it's the way he was brought up, but was I put on this earth to serve others? Come, my friend, come and sit down, let's talk a little about ourselves."

Mathieu wanted nothing more than to talk "about themselves," and he had the illusion that he had been there, sitting at Madame d'Argenti's side, for a long time, as he gave in to the lethargy brought on by wine and the hour – for Madame d'Argenti herself had explained that the noon hour "inclined one to sensual pleasures" – and asked whether he enjoyed sensual pleasures. "Which one?" he asked foolishly, for he knew so many kinds; he was about to speak of his love for old stones and sculptures when Madame d'Argenti silenced him by putting a finger to his lips and he breathed in the tranquility of chaste signs of affection that were hesitant, still unexpressed; he envied Antoine d'Argenti, who had had this woman at his side since awakening that morning, and he allowed her hand to rest on his knee as they sank slowly into the sofa cushions.

"What a pretty handbag," she said; "you must be very fond of me already, in your fashion, to offer me such a gift. But you'll ruin yourself on my account, it's really rather senseless. You'll see, I'm quite unworthy."

But despite her joy Madame d'Argenti still did not want to give up any oysters, so she daintily placed them in her own mouth with one hand as she fed Mathieu with the other; this movement of exchange or of engagement through food was endowed with such grace that Mathieu felt an instinct to suck her fingers; he did so, but she was so hungry she scarcely noticed. Mathieu wondered if Antoine d'Argenti was as sensitive as he to the feline aromas with which the cushions and the sofa had at some time been strongly inundated; but this petrified natural perfume also evoked the perfume of love. He had often been accused of having "too discriminating a nose," and it might have been true, for he was sensitive too, less agreeably, to the smell of fish, "the cats' fish," that was being cooked, unattended, in the kitchen. Madame d'Argenti did not suffer on account of these odours, however, and perhaps, Mathieu thought, she shared with her husband an Olympian insensitivity that made them impervious to any odour "from the lower regions," that animal dwelling which he, Mathieu, had always inhabited. That, he thought, was "the true royalty of the aristocrats of the spirit"; they no longer smelled anything at all.

"Are you a man?" asked Madame d'Argenti.

"Ah, indeed yes," he replied, filled with affirmation, "but couldn't we eat first?"

"In Paris one is always in a hurry, that's something you must learn immediately. There's the danger that Antoine might come back at any moment, and I have an appointment with my coiffeur at two o'clock."

"But Antoine, that's precisely . . . "

"Ah, but Antoine understands everything."

"Everything? Does he really?"

"About me, yes, he understands everything, absolutely everything. But what's wrong with you? You're rather well put together; do you find anything to criticize about me?"

"Tell me a little about you," Mathieu asked.

"Tell you about me? But I don't have time, and anything one might say can be accomplished more quickly with caresses, don't you think?"

Madame d'Argenti's caresses were incendiary and Mathieu Lelièvre, who thought himself quite experienced with girls his own age, in his country, was suddenly, abroad, reduced to the timid state of novice apprenticeship; Yvonne's effusions, which he had not expected so soon, especially not during a meal, took his breath away; he was vexed because he had not initiated their undressing before she did, and he began to talk about literature at a moment when chatter was forbidden. He observed as they were diligently making love, "for remember, Antoine might arrive at any moment," that Madame d'Argenti was one of those rare beings "who like sexual pleasure for its own sake, quite unadorned"; and if their enjoyment was rather brisk, "taken in haste, between two telephone calls," it mattered little to Madame d'Argenti and those like her, for they could play the entire series of scales indefinitely and, on various occasions, in the course of a single day. Mathieu, however, belonged to the opposite species, one that was less common; he belonged, he thought, to "the race of thinking sensualists," a race with awesome requirements and calculations, one that liked to extend its reveries over long reaches of time, to measure and weigh its impressions with radiant slowness. As Madame d'Argenti had no time to waste, she did not abandon herself to such moments of ecstasy; pleasure flew from her like a fly heading for some fiery horizon where it would be immediately extinguished in the clamour of death.

"Couldn't you postpone your appointment with the hairdresser?" Mathieu sighed. "Then we'd have several hours to ourselves."

"Oh no, that's simply not done. And I'd forgotten – the maid – yes. We've found a maid, Portuguese this time, and she arrives today."

He wanted to tell her how much he liked her velvety cheeks, her round shoulders, he wanted to grow drunk with words describing her entire person, embracing her anew with words; but she had disappeared into the bathroom and, as he bent over their lunch, he saw that the abundance of their Roman meal – the sixteen oysters, the cheese, the wine – all these marvels had been devoured by his slender ogre, but he had only now noticed it. "A fantastic woman," he thought, "the nobility of her appetites, her love of life – it's phenomenal!" and indulging his customary laziness he dozed in the hollow of the cushions, no longer troubled by odours, serene once more because of the feline memories in this house that, who knows, marked forever some part of Madame d'Argenti's past.

Mathieu Lelièvre danced his way home; he crossed streets heedless of cars and the cars were heedless of him. "Like any thinking sensualist" his memory returned several times to Madame d'Argenti's body as he thought sorrowfully that while he was still trembling from the sensual waves of their caresses she most likely had already forgotten him, as she offered up her hair and the nape of her neck to the hands of her coiffeur. Since she admitted that she had another appointment towards the end of the afternoon, she would go on forgetting until night.

"Try to understand, my friend, I'm busy, very busy. Ah!

and I have a sick friend I must visit before dinner. *Mon Dieu,* the life one leads in Paris – it's not like your land, with all those prairies and lakes. There one has time to live."

Mathieu thought of Antoine d'Argenti with misgivings, but they were feeble, for his love for Madame d'Argenti already occupied too large a place. Did she see Mathieu as a man like any other, or had she perceived that he refused any part of the brutal aspects of his sex? Even if this made of him a singular being – and it was not the only source of his singularity, he told himself – Mathieu often spoke out, even before his friends, thereby drawing the chilly judgement of Pierre-Henri Lajeunesse, against "the sort of virility that is expressed on this earth by war and violence; and it's we men who have always, throughout History, been the authors of such massacres, it is we who have always expressed our virile supremacy in that manner." Once he confessed his pacifism, it did not foster greater peace and serenity about him but, rather, aroused a combative, warlike mood in his friends and, what Mathieu most abhorred, "that need to prove how virile they are," even in the course of a simple discussion. As fate would have it, Mathieu Lelièvre was an only child, although he would have liked so much "to have a sister to protect and defend against the warlike savages we are." He hoped, then, to show Madame d'Argenti how much consideration there was in his love for her, and if it happened that he was "a carnivore like the others" it was quite unintentional, and perhaps due to "the vice of masculine domination" that had been germinating in him for centuries. Mathieu was a gentle man, which did not create a good reputation for him, but he was unaware how little concern Madame d'Argenti had for his own sense of himself. "I've always liked the strength of young men," she had told him as she looked in the mirror to ensure that her own image had not been rubbed too vigorously by the young faun who had just unexpectedly entered her life, something she found rather delicious, for she loathed routine, and Mathieu had immediately interpreted her words as a compliment to his amorous vigour. "But perhaps she knows how much I respect her too," he thought, and he was so convinced of Madame d'Argenti's fragility that he was quite astonished when she abruptly relinquished a final embrace in order to take one athletic leap to the door, greet the maid and peremptorily begin to give her orders in a voice that was suddenly authoritarian.

"Ah, so it's you. We've been expecting you; get right to work, there's a great deal to do. My husband needs clean socks for tonight and could you wash my son's underwear too? Ah yes, I agree, a disgusting boy indeed, he's been hiding them under the refrigerator for a good month now, have you ever seen such a boy? It's a childhood habit, I can't do a thing about it, I've never had time to take care of him, to say nothing of the desire. Ah yes, there's two weeks ironing too, I'm sorry to ask you for so much, but it's urgent, we've been waiting for you for several days . . . Oh yes, and what is your name?"

"Bonita."

"Bonita, what a pretty name, it evokes all the delights of your country. Bonita! Well, child, since we must – off to work!"

Could it be, Mathieu wondered, that this family was clean only on the outside, that it was capable of secretly committing such sins against hygiene? Bonita seemed overwhelmed by the harvest awaiting her.

"Where shall I begin, Madame?"

"Do everything at once, it's easier that way."

"No, it's we who carry cleanliness too far," Mathieu went on thinking; "these people are too well educated to spend all their time under the shower, looking for dirt, that's all!" And he told himself that beneath the patina of their aromatic and polished culture, the d'Argentis had no need to wash. They were enemies of soap, "of the entire American civilization with its perpetual cleaning and scrubbing," Mathieu Lelièvre thought again, they were above any perfume because they still possessed the odour of the past and so they could slip, as into a mould, into made-to-measure English suits or any other classic garb whose price and quality suited them extraordinarily well. But Mathieu did not yet know that in this respect Madame d'Argenti was quite unlike those people his friends called disrespectfully, *"maudits Français"*; no, Madame d'Argenti, mother of two sons who would have considered it degrading to be caught in a bathtub, liked water and even went so far as to regret not having a swimming pool in her house. Mathieu, once again, had been wounded in his love of France by the label *"maudits Français"* and he found it strange that the Québecois, so quick to take offence where they themselves were concerned, intolerant of any such flagellation, would be capable of inventing this expression which he considered so bigoted. Pierre-Henri Lajeunesse had explained to him, however, that there was a "rough sort of affection in the term *maudit Français* that was so often repeated" it became a kind of teasing that was both mordant and inviting, according to Pierre-Henri, and that "anyone who understands this is already one of us." But as soon as Mathieu arrived in Paris he had observed that the *"maudit Français"* that might be a sign of intercontinental kinship when one was in Quebec was, in France, a rigid insult that cut off any hope of friendship. "Ah! I know, you call me a *'maudit Français'*," the taxi driver, already feeling threatened by his fare, had told him as he drove in from Orly, and sullenly he rushed to deposit at the door of his hotel this foreign cousin who even as he spoke the man's own language insulted him along the way, tossing several metaphors and a great deal of acid in his face. Mathieu attached himself to taxi drivers as though they were disparate fragments of France that he was seeking, asking each one a geographical question: "So you're from the Auvergne? I love the Auvergne . . . " and so forth, believing that by doing so he would stimulate cascades of information, descriptions of mountains and torrents; but whether it was the shadow of the term *maudit Français* that suddenly crossed the driver's mind or his irritation at driving across Paris, the an-

31

cestor from the Auvergne preserved until the present did not answer Mathieu Lelièvre; he grumbled frequently about the weather or simply said nothing at all, considering that he was entitled to the anarchy of silence that not even a loquacious Québecois was going to disturb. Mathieu, however, was unwilling to admit failure and, beaten on one side, he carved out a place for himself on the other. It was a singular distinction, for when everyone else returned from Paris they complained they had made no friends among the *maudits Français* while he, after a few weeks, had formed an entire cortège of *"Français aimables,"* friends for a moment or an hour whom he would remember all his life. But his liaison with Madame d'Argenti took place on another level, far from the streets and cafés, far from the people he loved; it was a liaison that involved someone besides himself – the "observer" he had talked about to Pierre-Henri and the "French quintessence"; it was an affair in a world of which he knew nothing but of which he could expect and perhaps dread a great deal as well, for although Madame d'Argenti had become his mistress he was still painfully in her thrall. His passion was rekindled as soon as he left her. Where was she going? What was she doing – and most of all, what was she doing when she was alone, during idle hours? It was exasperating, Mathieu thought, to have a woman entirely to oneself, one who gave herself to you with loyal shamelessness for the time of a comet to pass through the sky, only to see her dash off into the Paris fog, looking like someone just going shopping but actually leaving behind her, as she moved on to other pleasures, her cape swaying in the wind, delicious but appeased emotions that were for her devoid of interest, exhausted pleasures of which her lover imagined himself still the master, but which she had stopped thinking about. But Madame d'Argenti had reassured Mathieu by giving him a key to her private apartment, so routines had been established, so soon, Mathieu thought, and every evening – at the hour when he felt that he possessed all Paris simply by looking at it, when the roofs seemed to melt in an orange and pink luminosity (his contemplation of the death throes of objects was often interrupted by the strident groaning of cars on the streets) – he climbed the stairs to Yvonne d'Argenti's room, where she was waiting and so to the happiness of events yet to come.

"Don't be offended, my friend, if I go out into my world without you, for the moment; it's because it's so sweet to see you again after being with those fashionable, disillusioned people. Our often cruel society might very well make fun of your freshness and youth, but we'll go out together soon, you'll see."

But what was her "world," Mathieu Lelièvre wondered? When Madame d'Argenti dropped languidly onto her bed she seemed to him to come from the midst of a social extravaganza where everything appeared to be vast and beautiful. "Ah! such wine, such meals! Such friends!" she would sigh, and it seemed that there still drifted through the air and about her half-unclothed body a carnal attraction that had entered the room with her, even stronger than the one her rather sleepy presence aroused in Mathieu . . . He began to grow accustomed, too, to the decadent gift she made of herself when she came in from these evenings, decadent, he thought, because while feigning sleep she would savour, beneath her lashes, other dreams and other images, while her body coupled freely and joyously with her present lover, becoming increasingly frenzied and bereft. Was he, then, jealous of her thoughts?

"What marvellous energy, my friend, but forgive me; I'm falling asleep."

Mathieu observed once again that his excessive energy was particularly unbecoming. Even when he was a child, his parents would reproach him for being too healthy and zealous; at the age of nine he had cut open a friend's forehead because he "wanted to show him how to shovel a snowbank in five minutes"; at twelve, he broke a bone in his grandmother's elbow by introducing her to "a baseball game" in the cellar at home; his whole existence was generously filled with incidents of the sort. He was, as his mother said, one of those "who spill over the top" and he had left behind, from his school years, a reputation as a troublemaker for which he was sorry today, as he believed himself particularly endowed for reflection and analysis.

"Alas!" he mused, "who in this world truly knows you?"

"Don't think, though," Madame d'Argenti added, "that I'm refusing my pleasure; no, in fact I'm beginning to appreciate you more and more." Nonetheless, after uttering these words in a voice that was wide awake, Madame d'Argenti gave in to sleep. In a few moments, Mathieu thought, she will no longer inhabit her body, she will be dreaming. All was silence and an almost religious atmosphere followed the disorder of passion. That, he thought, was passion: a sleeping woman, articles of clothing on a chair, the half light; it was this "atmosphere," as closed as an egg, born of the other and of oneself, in which the last rites of the celebration – silence, sleep – ended in melancholy. But at that moment the everyday world burst in in all its glory: a breeze came through the open window and the cat, returning from his evening stroll across the roofs, jumped from the window to the bed, spreading around him as he quivered and landed all the odours of autumn, the night and its damp perfume with which his paws and tail were still impregnated. "Victor, Victor Hugo, Hugo my darling Victor," Mathieu murmured, filled with gratitude towards the old cat that had suddenly appeared, but the grey Persian seducer (whose name was, in fact, Victorine, but as Madame d'Argenti did not like either the female sex or the maternal duties attached to it, even so far as Victorine's animal existence was concerned, she had rigorously corrected this error of nature's) did not like Mathieu; only Madame d'Argenti could call him Hugo as she stroked the nape of his neck, and he looked at Mathieu with a large and wrathful eye: who was this intruder who shared his mistress's bed? The cat was the treasure of Madame d'Argenti's sentimental archives, weary of everything,

34

and he tolerated, not without pain, any misdemeanours by the woman who thought herself responsible for him but of whom the cat undoubtedly considered himself to be the only true moral guardian, the sole overseer whose wisdom everyone ignored, so much that he had become – he whose affection was sober, his principles severe – one of those animals, witness and king, Mathieu had first seen in French paintings, at a woman's feet; not a dignified, rebellious cat but a complacent cat, obliging judge and jury who closed his eyes or went out the window while his friend abandoned herself – in his eyes – to her sinner's ravings. Madame d'Argenti slept eloquently and the cat now seemed to be saying: "I'm here, I'm protecting her, why don't you leave?" and Mathieu thought this warning was, in its way, an order. It often began with Victor clawing the blanket and then when Mathieu got up to dress, it would continue with increasingly playful, liberating purring, until once Mathieu had tiptoed out of the room the cat could no longer conceal its delight and in one leap he would go to "his place" on Madame d'Argenti's shoulder. Mathieu would have to wait until the next evening to discover the warmth of this exquisite place and while he waited, he was pierced by the cold as he walked around the windy island; for, accustomed as he was to the cold of winter, he would have preferred one of his own country's fierce storms to the wisp of fog that encircled him with anguish, as much spiritual as physical, once he had crossed the Pont-Neuf, as though when leaning over the Seine during the night he had heard some call, stifled by the waves, and found in it the deprivation of solitude. He recalled a tragedy Madame d'Argenti claimed to have forgotten, but this tragedy, Mathieu thought, was the first one they had experienced together: as they were coming home from an afternoon movie they had seen, in the very place where Mathieu stopped every night, contemplating this memory, a drowned man being pulled from the muddy water, whose pale and swollen face had often come back to him.

"But don't look, my friend, you know very well it upsets you. Come now, I must stop at the pastry shop."

"But it's a man."

"It was, my friend, it was . . . I confess I find that mass of swollen white flesh highly repugnant. Now don't look; come now, such things happen here often. Ah! it's dreadful, they must use ropes to bring the corpse to the surface. I can understand why you're moved, but what's the use?"

What had particularly upset Mathieu, however, was the reverence, the mute respect of the blue-clad workmen who sent their ropes searching to the bottom of the water, like the apostles of the resurrection, but this was a resurrection of the most neglected of the unknown – a man stiff and ravaged and put to death more than once by the passage of the water and the seasons; he was a man whose very features had been washed away or forgotten, his smile had dissolved, but still they greeted him at the surface of the world – and thereby returned him to themselves and the vitality of their everyday existence. Mathieu Lelièvre suddenly thought that the man's death should be compared with the return of a living being, rather than the devastated fish he'd mistaken it for. In an hour or two the workers would probably have lost their merciful grace and, far from representing angels at the grave, they would be once again simply what they usually were – men indifferent to other's misfortunes, brutal and stingy. For Mathieu, however, who still had a glimmer of common goodness in his mind, the fresco often returned from the depths of the dark water, and he would remember the drowned man he had mourned in silence, without tears or voice, confused with the men pulling to the shore on their ropes the heavy and outrageous weight of a man buried in the river alone with his death.

Like many people who sleep at night, Madame d'Argenti imagined that the day ended with her. Mathieu would certainly have surprised her very much if he had told her he began to live at the very moment she entered the series of lives of her dreams, closing her eyes to "the world" until morning. Often when Mathieu was walking along the streets of Paris at night he would have liked to remember a moment of abandon between Madame d'Argenti and himself that was not only sexual, but such moments were rare; until now their complicity was mainly sensual and Madame d'Argenti never said to Mathieu the words he waited for impatiently every night: "My friend, if you only knew how much I need you!" Nor did she ask him in a burst of amorous investigation: "Who are you really? When will you tell me all about yourself?" Mathieu was surprised to be sharing a woman's bed while they remained strangers. It is true that she had sobbed in his arms as she told him how much suffering her children had caused her, how much her husband had hurt her, but in his selfishness Mathieu was dissatisfied to hear her speak of her husband and children more than of himself, and sorry too to see how quickly Madame d'Argenti had wiped her round eyes and begun to talk about a dress she wished to buy, her light, childlike laugh chasing away all the concerned gravity she had stirred up in Mathieu's soul. Still, he thought, even though she gave herself to him entirely, Madame d'Argenti enjoyed her secrets. Wandering through Paris as he did was delicious, but loving caused him pain. What was the good of being apart from Madame d'Argenti only to find himself with her again in memory? He was more attached to these memories, still green, than to all the beauty of Paris at night; and he who had waited so long to use his eyes to admire this city, could admire and see only the woman whom he carried in his heart. That evening she had shown him old photographs and children's drawings she had kept for years, in a basket by her bed. "I've been so unhappy because of them; if you only knew. It's true that I've abandoned them, poor things, but I wasn't born to be a mother or to look after others. Many adults are like that, but they discover it too late. I think passion can turn us all quite evil." "What passion? What kind of love can make us so wicked?" Mathieu wanted to ask; he on the contrary had felt he was becoming better since meeting Madame d'Argenti, and he wanted to share with the entire world the amorous games of this compelling virtue. "You've had other lovers then, even in the early years of your marriage with Antoine?" Mathieu wanted to add as well, but Yvonne d'Argenti was already talking about something else so coldly that she seemed no longer to be addressing him but rather herself or Antoine. This dismayed Mathieu, as he could be receptive to only one mood at a time, not to this perpetual switching from hot to cold, from tender to biting, that seemed to be Madame d'Argenti's natural state. She also had the gift of surprising Mathieu by suddenly announcing as they were making love that she had to "pay an urgent visit to a countess, and if I don't take you with me this time, my friend, it's because I know how boring you would find that sort of dinner," or by promptly getting up to look for her shoe in a corner of the bedroom, thereby indicating – she who constantly told Mathieu how much she loved pleasure – that she was more greedy than voluptuous and that basically, perhaps, she was contemptuous of the aspect of passion he was so attached to – repose, the intimacy of two beings who, instead of this provincial serenity, "this strange way of seeing love" that was Mathieu's, preferred the bustle of Paris and the festive air that seemed at any hour to arouse Madame d'Argenti to such nervous expectation. Sometimes she would say to Mathieu: "Aren't you flattered that I like making love with you so much, even if it's often rather rushed?" and Mathieu told himself that such raw sincerity might mask a chaste soul.

"Why should you and I not love each other for other reasons?" she would ask as well. "You'll see, I'll be good for you, I'll introduce you to all the delights of Paris."

"And Antoine?" Mathieu inquired belatedly; would this insolent, amoral liaison wound him? For Mathieu had the illusion that he need only speak of his "amoral liaison with Madame d'Argenti" and he would experience remorse he didn't really feel, not even before Antoine whom he was able to forget for days, as one forgets the face of a man seen in a dream. How could he be so insensitive? Was it the crime of forgetfulness, fruit of passion, that Madame d'Argenti had told him of when she spoke about her children?

"Antoine?" she replied, "have you seen nothing, my friend? Antoine likes young boys, it's obvious to anyone who has eyes – women too, of course . . . At least he loved me once! ah, so briefly! It is so hard to be rejected for one of those young thugs, so often . . . He's never compromised me; if you only knew! I was hungry too, believe me; one's sex can languish from hunger just like any other organ. What, fundamentally, did I need in life? Love. Yes, that's it, that's all. Yet always, it's the only thing that we're refused!"

"Young boys?" Mathieu Lelièvre asked, his voice quavering, for he told himself that in her conjugal disappointment Madame d'Argenti had most likely committed some irredeemable calumny towards her husband. "No, it isn't possible, you must be mistaken."

"What do you mean? Are you suggesting I don't know my husband?"

Mathieu thought that even if Madame d'Argenti had personal reasons for speaking of her husband to her lover in that way, loyalty to Antoine – if not discretion – would have kept her from making such a confession. But she became suddenly quick to take offence. "All the same – replace me with a young boy, such poor taste!" she murmured, and from her gentle, childlike profile which Mathieu had contemplated an hour earlier, her "pillow profile" as he called it – even though there was no pillow on Madame d'Argenti's bed, for she had told him that mountains made her dizzy, that she liked only water and flat land, that she dreaded any elevation – from that gentle profile there emerged for a moment another one, as sharp as Madame d'Argenti, who was grumbling about "those boys of Antoine's," punctuating her remarks with "how much pain they too had caused her"; but she soon tempered her indignation with a smile, and in a movement of tenderness Mathieu rediscovered all the seductiveness of the woman he loved.

"You're very young, my friend," said Madame d'Argenti, kissing Mathieu noisily and hastily, "and if you want to become a writer you have a lot to learn; you have a great deal of imagination but you don't know much about men." "But I *am* a writer," Mathieu wanted to declare, though pride held him back. His features were marked briefly by irritation, but although Mathieu observed all of Madame d'Argenti's moods, she was often insensitive to his.

"Speaking of Antoine, my friend, everyone is aware, or has been for a long time; only someone as ingenuous as you wouldn't notice.

"Poor Antoine," Mathieu thought, "another man betrayed by his wife!" Mathieu seemed unaware that by refusing to learn the truth from the charming, treacherous lips of Madame d'Argenti, "this truth, my truth, which is always true but which changes constantly," as she said, he was also refusing to change his own image of Antoine, an image he was fond of.

"I understand everything," he said indifferently; "one must understand everything in life."

But he disappointed himself; was he not, like so many others once they are exposed to directions in life different from their own, a victim of what he most hated – prejudice? You couldn't know, he thought, nor could you foresee what form prejudice would take, or its species or its silent ripening in people's minds, nor at what moment in contact with a real event something that was only a prejudice would become bigotry. As Mathieu Lelièvre had never before given a thought to Antoine d'Argenti's habits, busy as he was experiencing his own, he had only today discovered that where Antoine was concerned he had always cherished "that poisonous mistrust of anything different from oneself, which is the basis of intolerance." Mathieu reassured himself by thinking that in this affair Antoine would have the consolation of not feeling any jealousy. He began to appreciate his kindness, his discretion. Antoine d'Argenti would often invite Mathieu into his room, which was always filled with shadows and smoke; his nonchalant sons would run to him as soon as he came back from his office in the evening; Mathieu and Antoine would clink their glasses of scotch and when it was time to "go up to Yvonne" they would take leave of each other with distant affection. Mathieu had always been grateful for this distance, which he attributed to the rigidity of the virile ties between himself and the man he still called "Monsieur d'Argenti."

Ah! how disturbing for him was this hour that sounded in the darkened apartment. Mathieu – perhaps because he described the hour as "hollow" – felt as though he were descending into self-disillusionment; he who an hour before had adored himself was suddenly, now, reproaching himself for his banality, the banality of being a slave to his senses, he thought; and it was with this feeling of discontent that he went up to see Madame d'Argenti, sometimes prepared for a long wait. He had come to Paris intending to write a masterpiece, "to work like a horse," as he had written to Pierre-Henri, but what was he doing besides work lazily with his body? He loved intensely, but all the same it was not much. "You and I suffer from the same malady," Antoine told him; "we both like to burn." But did he burn enough? Thereafter Mathieu became Antoine's confidant, and it was in listening to Antoine speak of "the passion that devours" that Mathieu saw that he loved Madame d'Argenti "with a fire that was too gentle." He had been unable to praise his mistress in language both precise and discreet, and most of all full of imagery, of which Antoine was a master when he was glorifying the beauty of boys. Antoine showed Mathieu how an artist of the word can say anything, even name and describe "young boys' asses" as he paid them true homage – as a dazzled naturalist might speak of his flowers or his bees. Mathieu stammered something about "Madame d'Argenti's grace, the subtlety of her wit," then he would stop, fearing he might add to the portrait he wished to paint of Yvonne d'Argenti for her husband the few flaws in her personality that he had managed to perceive.

"Yvonne is violent and sensual, but you'll see, my friend, she's worthy of your love. In any case we know, you and I, we know that in this life any love is a miracle."

Thus spoke Antoine who guessed everything, Mathieu thought. How pleasant it was to hear him talk of everything, "of Madame d'Argenti's whims and moral disarray." Only this man, this finely shaded husband could, even as he amassed clusters of rhetorical figures, celebrate a woman so majestically, with a respect that was almost lyrical and with the tranquillity of intimate knowledge. Listening to Antoine d'Argenti was rather like watching him paint the picture in which Mathieu felt he was living, with Antoine as well as his wife. The thought comforted Mathieu as he waited for Madame d'Argenti in her room.

"And you'll understand soon enough, my friend, that Yvonne's ardent animal nature can only be good for you. It will help you dispel the excesses of youth and besides, it will be your first lesson in fashionable society."

"Why have you renounced her? Is it because you love her?"

"Ah, because she's insatiable, my friend, insatiable! By the way, Mathieu, allow me to suggest a list of small gifts, which would please her so much, that I cannot offer her this year. Perhaps you know that one of my sons is studying at one of the most expensive schools in France . . . and my daughter is in a lycée in London . . . I am, in a word, in debt, all because of my wife's whims!" he added bitterly, but he then began, with a gentleness filled with even greater emotion, to describe his wife's needs that he was unable to fill. "Yes, you remember . . . those gloves . . . You saw them with her at Hermès; and the perfume she likes, yes, the price isn't really excessive, is it?"

But Antoine d'Argenti didn't say: "I ask you in the name of my wife"; on the contrary, his voice was stripped of all authority. It was merely a humble request from a man who was tired but in love; and Mathieu, touched by this modesty, could only reply: "But of course, Antoine, you're right, these trinkets cost practically nothing and, as you say, they give Yvonne such pleasure."

"Have you received the advance from your publisher, then? I hope it was generous."

"No, but I'll be getting it soon. They promised."

"Don't forget that Yvonne intends to tell her critic friends about your book, so you won't be completely overlooked."

"Yes, that's very kind of her. I don't know how to thank her," said Mathieu.

After dwelling on the hope that he "would not be completely forgotten by the Paris literary set," Mathieu loved Madame d'Argenti even more fervently. Yesterday, he thought he loved her, but today he venerated her. Why not, then, buy her, in addition to the gloves and perfume, the woollen blanket for autumn nights she had so dreamed about? It was Victor the cat who hoped to receive this gift; he had worn out all of Madame d'Argenti's blankets with his intransigent claws.

At times Madame d'Argenti would sigh: "Poor cat, he'll be cold!" Mathieu cared little about the anemic state of his finances. He thought that once his book was published all his cares would fly away. With her divine lack of concern, Madame d'Argenti had taught him to believe in magic. As he sipped his scotch in Antoine's room that evening, Mathieu thought of Madame d'Argenti's children: were they indeed those whose past, according to their mother, was filled with so much debris? Did she exaggerate somewhat her maternal guilt? Whenever Mathieu encountered the shadows of Paul or Christian prowling around their father in the silent apartment he wondered if Madame d'Argenti had told him the whole truth about her children after all, this woman who said of herself that she was the enemy of "every baby in the world before the age of eleven," the same one who, like a specialist in the adversities of childhood, would quote

Freud to her friends as soon as the tiny pearl of her progeny's first tooth appeared through its tears and she became the very incarnation of motherhood, offering, from the cradle on, milk and doctrine, a form of maternal love so sophisticated that Mathieu suddenly doubted his own mother who was not only ignorant of psychology but had never been afraid when she was bringing up her son to use the most rudimentary means, such as the one she called "the clout that'll clear your head" and "the scolding that builds character." Or was it simply that today's Pauls and Christians had not learned to survive the memory of their humiliations? As for Antoine, Mathieu could reproach him only for loving his sons too much, for maintaining, along with his rights as a father, a lover's demands as well; but it seemed quite understandable in light of Antoine's physical and intellectual seductiveness. How many times had he witnessed Paul's adoring attitude towards his father as soon as the latter opened his mouth . . . Christian was always dozing in a corner or sprawled sensuously on the dusty carpet with the cat, his position evoking – and how it would have surprised him! – Madame d'Argenti in bed and her feline aggressiveness as she waited; it was a sight that Mathieu contemplated with never-ending delight. Paul, with military stiffness, stood by his father and, without seeming to understand them, approved of his philosophical definitions. His approval seemed to be transmitted to his strong jaw, as though to say: "Yes, mon Colonel!" "Illiterate," his mother would say of him, but Mathieu Lelièvre thought it unfair, for Paul, like all those who live in the kitchen and seldom leave the house, was submissive, one of those pale cooks worn out by the servitude essential to satisfy other people's greed; and if he was puerile and dreamy it was perhaps because he had been entrusted with feeding all the hungers of the household. Mathieu thought that in time, as the years passed over Paul's long sloping neck, the boy would become a replica of his father, but a replica more indistinct than the present, still solid, Antoine d'Argenti whom Mathieu saw before him every evening. Antoine derived his stability, his reality, from what Madame d'Argenti never named without emotion "Sensual Pleasure." Antoine d'Argenti must devote a good deal of time to preparations for his amorous conquests in order to present such an appearance! Whether he was at his piano playing Schumann, or ensconced in his easy chair with a book, he seemed to radiate a fiercely contained passion, to be independent when those about him were not, so that his entire being seemed to announce: "I am preparing for Beauty." And Mathieu, who could admire – again through the deceptive illusion of photographs – the beauty of the adolescents Antoine loved, began to understand that even such a reasonable man could be made giddy by a pretty face. How had he, Mathieu Lelièvre, been able to live through various periods of his life without being aware that Beauty exists? Men like Antoine would become frantic in order to possess two slender legs ready to frolic in the fields, "for the little mask, almost ascetic, sometimes purified to the point of transparency that will never return, that is the face of a young boy" as Antoine d'Argenti said. (And as Mathieu looked at the photographs on the piano, nothing could be more strikingly precise.) Yes, serious men might die for this moment of grace but meanwhile, what had he, Mathieu, seen behind people's faces except "moods and more moods"? It was disappointing. Many faces had also numbed him, so repelled was he at the frequent sight of a low forehead, indicating foolishness – but he dared not speak of that to Antoine.

"It's possible to see things in very different ways," he said modestly.

"You'll see," Antoine replied, "Paris will be very good for you. You'll be able to appreciate what is beautiful and great here."

Touched by Mathieu's generosity, Madame d'Argenti now invited him into "her world" and he was quick to write his parents (for that was another thing that made him peculiar in his friends' eyes: Mathieu Lelièvre loved his parents and spoke of them only with admiration) that he had dined "in the most beautiful apartments in Paris," for everything had suddenly become beautiful for him: he loved a beautiful woman, etc.; while in his letters to Pierre-Henri Lajeunesse, which he embellished with aesthetic effusions, behind the halo of beauty which he cast over every head, even his own, behind the gilt and carving of the barons and marquis he had visited, other images, less ornate, crossed his mind. He thought of Bonita scrubbing Paul's underwear, grimy antiques according to Madame d'Argenti who spoke with all objective severity; this underwear had its own secret history, far removed from any salon, almost "the intimacy of a soul" Mathieu thought. For Bonita had murmured when she saw the garments: "No, Madame, I can't do that!" expressing in an outburst of indignant nobility that she could not touch such things. "I've got a lot of friends now, *mon vieux*," Mathieu wrote to Pierre-Henri, but though his pen was insolent, his heart was troubled. At one of those dinners Madame d'Argenti had introduced Mathieu to her friends in the following manner:

"He's a young writer from a young country, so you must forgive him a great many things. I've decided to help him, for we must take risks in this life, mustn't we?" And yet he had regained his confidence when he saw Madame d'Argenti bring her fleshy lips close to the silver cup she was holding; it was as though the sparkle of beauty he sought everywhere was saving him now from any painful rejection, even making him somewhat deaf to insults. When his hosts treated him with veiled contempt (but was the word contempt appropriate for such creatures? Was it not, rather, a supreme lack of interest to which he was not accustomed, one of those differences between the two continents?), when by chance some malicious word (but who knows, perhaps it was unintentional?) embarrassed him, to avoid listening to it he would look ecstatically towards his host and marvel at "what was so fundamentally beautiful" in the eye that stared at him or at some shocking detail of his person that "was not pleasing." Was it his accent, or had he once again overdone the eau de cologne? But the lethal expression of an old count or a young princess – he had noticed that these looks sprang from the same source when they descended upon you with the authority of privilege – the look, with the same forced but cold fever, was about to attack someone else, usually a female guest who could scarcely be seen, as she was all wrapped in herself and her own fearful shadow. Relieved, Mathieu turned to Madame d'Argenti. What did the years separating them matter when he saw her youthful cheeks? Did she not still have the angelic smile of their first meeting, the smile of her photographs as a young girl? True, she was not always as seductive as during these evenings with her friends. It even happened, as it happens to every angel, that she smashed plates, stamping on her cutlery with her eternal rage, but this only made her more fascinating. At times the clamour was intended mainly to stifle the piano sonata Antoine was playing, but she would regret such fits of rage. "Ah!" she would exclaim, running to her husband's arms, "Antoine, my dearest Antoine, forgive me! If you only knew how I need to be forgiven!"

"I forgive you," he would reply drily, and Mathieu would see again the radiant smile, the liquid freshness of her teeth offered up for a kiss and he would be astonished to see Antoine d'Argenti decline all these gifts and slam the piano shut.

On weekends, Mathieu would go with the d'Argenti family to the country. It was at their property in Normandy that he met Etienne, one of Antoine's friends. The young man, Mathieu's age, no longer received the same compliments from Antoine he once had, but Antoine still treated him affectionately, with a certain courteous reserve that was a sacred virtue between the two friends and one for which they shared a tacit respect, for when Etienne spoke about Antoine to Mathieu he always called him "Antoine d'Argenti," keeping behind perfectly shaped lips any other,

47

said to Paul; but Madame d'Argenti's son looked down and said nothing.

"You like music and so do I; we could talk about our favourite musicians."

Paul never spoke of music or musicians without consulting his father. He was silent. Meanwhile, Madame d'Argenti was impatiently awaiting the steak for lunch: they knew she was always impatient at that hour, so why did they make her wait? Even Victor could take no more. He showed his approval by rubbing himself in a familiar way against Madame d'Argenti's leg, while his mistress, with a hand that was small but unbelievably vigorous, bent the teeth of the forks. Later, Mathieu would eat without appetite, while Madame d'Argenti cut the meat with her communicant's teeth. Mathieu, still filled with love for this woman, felt no hunger because it seemed as though he had already eaten with her, and seeing her after such a meal with her appetite intensified seemed to disturb him, for he could not take his eyes off the pink cavern of her throat.

"I've told you before," Monsieur d'Argenti said to Mathieu, "in that respect we're the same; we like to consume ourselves . . . You're burning, my friend, that's good . . . But eat something anyway." Absentmindedly, Mathieu thought of the "two mouths" in Madame d'Argenti's body, of which she spoke to him profusely; this should have gone on to cast some searching light over his mind, but Christian came in from a motorcycle race through the woods, his jacket spotted with grease, and he was like a vision of reality Mathieu needed so much, in so many ways. Why was life not more often such a series of pictures, melancholy and poignant? For one could see again an endless succession of images that were no longer received, that would not return, as though they had been stored, hidden from the world in soft pillows a few moments earlier, in the distant scent of wild game and marshes, and it all came to you at the back of a room with the window open. It was already over, though Mathieu Lelièvre thought the hours passed too slowly. After lunch Paul

50

disappeared into his sound system, wearing the earphones he armed himself with as soon as meals were over – meals and their servility – and the crescendo of the music carried him far away. He who scraped the cat's mess off the tile floor and washed the leeks, became in turn solo performer and conductor. The greatness of genius passed through his eyes as his hand sadly beat time in the air; perhaps it was true after all, Mathieu thought, observing him surreptitiously, that Paul was the heir of an unhappy childhood.

"There is only the present," said Madame d'Argenti to her husband as they drank a *digestif* in the salon. "Haven't you always told me to forget the past? To think only of the present? Ah! I mustn't forget to tell Paul to feed the rabbits."

"Come now, he's entitled to a day off too."

"You've always preferred your children to your wife. *Mon Dieu*, Antoine, how I've suffered!"

"I know, I know."

Often, when he returned from the country, Mathieu Lelièvre would delight in going to the theatre with the d'Argentis. What saddened him, however, was the other scene that ended the day: Antoine and Etienne replacing their hunting clothes, still blood-stained, with evening dress, thereby becoming even more magnificent than they had been in the red aura of crimes committed in the forest, whereas Mathieu, like all other interchangeable creatures, remained the same, still wearing the same pullover. They would wait by the car like two deposed sophisticates in the rank of chauffeurs, for Madame d'Argenti, who loathed waiting but was never on time; she would finally arrive, desirable and desired by Mathieu who had never before seen her radiant in her black cape, slipping her arm into his as she said: "But my friend, do you not dress for the theatre where you come from? Come, don't be sad, I love you as you are . . . Oh, Etienne, how handsome you are this evening!"

Etienne turned his haughty profile towards Antoine d'Argenti, speaking in a low voice. Madame d'Argenti seemed to sense that the whispering harmony of this male friendship was some sort of iniquity and Mathieu noticed that she bit her lips furiously. And yet, Madame d'Argenti was responsible for a certain complicity with her husband against her own sex as she said with him, when she spotted at the back of the theatre a chorus of women wearing hats: "What are such women doing here?"

"Yes, it's frightful, and they're from the provinces too," Etienne said to Monsieur d'Argenti.

Mathieu Lelièvre looked at Antoine and Etienne, surprised and tormented as he suddenly became aware of the cracks in the still fresh tableaux formed by the people around him. What sort of world did they belong to? Was it his? These women, whom she called "plain," were rather like his own mother, with their awkward enthusiasm. They wore the same sort of hat, the kind that for women who are quite naturally wives and mothers affirms the sex (and the duties of that sex) that they represent with pride. And this is so even if they must wear it upon heads that have been "permanently" waved. Ah! Mathieu Lelièvre thought, how can the d'Argentis, who have been given everything by life, seize on the rare signs of pride, the rare pleasures of this group of women, plain bourgeois women perhaps, but too innocent even to conceal the expression of it? It is true the d'Argentis knew how to conceal everything. They seemed to be the bearers of a fragile past. Antoine, perhaps, still suffered when he thought of a journey he had taken to Egypt with the young Etienne, the one who could never again be spied behind his features. There had been so much passionate tenderness, so much of the young wolf's lascivious abandon, and now there was only Etienne's glacial present: how could physical love lose so much savour? Etienne was only twenty-one but he was already old, old in an Old World way, the Old World of France for which Mathieu had long felt such nostalgia and which was now disappointing him. It was probably because Mathieu could not bear Etienne's ideas, which seemed to come from the Middle Ages. Etienne would speak of how he missed "the lost colonies" and of how he regretted, too, "not having shed enough blood," notions Mathieu found intolerable, formulated as they were without feeling in the mouth of a modern child. But only he noticed the outrage: Monsieur and Madame d'Argenti, on the contrary, praised Etienne's intelligence: "It's sheer perversion to be both so intelligent and so splendid," she said. Nor was Antoine shocked at the offhanded contempt that flowed rhythmically like the lines of a poem written by a murderer, from the delicate mouth of a friend. But perhaps, Mathieu thought, Antoine listened only vaguely to the comments of the one he had loved, perhaps he was more preoccupied by the gentle dream of yesterday's "little boy" whom he still cherished in the silence of his memory, than by Etienne's political incoherence. No one knew how much Antoine d'Argenti had secretly suffered and wept for this boy who was lost to him and to his brothers, for those dazzling summers of desire tended to fade in time, he said, and old age would soon draw near. He often told Mathieu: "I'm getting old, the monastic period will soon be here. Of course there's still an unimaginable quantity of boys to love, but one must collect them, waken them gently – and I'm tired."

"If I were you I'd go to Tunisia," Etienne told Antoine, giving the *coup de grâce* with a malicious sparkle in his eyes; "you'd find everything there you might want."

"There are times, Etienne, when you don't know me at all," said Antoine. "If I brought a boy back from Tunisia it would be to offer him a better education, to save him, even if the word amuses you. I've always tried to educate my boys, to make life more pleasant for them. No Etienne, there are times when you misjudge even my manner of loving."

"Ah!" Etienne replied with a shrug, "we all love in the same way, just as we hunt in the same way."

Mathieu found that it wasn't always so easy to maintain the observer's imperturbable detachment. It was not only at the theatre, he thought, that the d'Argentis and their friend Etienne would exclaim: "Ah, such vulgar, unbearable people!" in voices sharpened for the ceremony of disdain, but in restaurants or any other place where people assembled too; it seemed that the d'Argentis would condemn to damnation an entire section of working-class France. Perhaps, who knows, it was all simply a question of education, perhaps that was done in Paris. Madame d'Argenti would say of her husband that he had once "worn white gloves to groom horses," that he was inconsolable at "having lost his valet because, you understand, my friend, with the life we lead we can no longer afford to live as he did when he was younger." What seemed haughtiness to Mathieu then, was perhaps only the natural effect of an elite education, apart from the rest of the world. What did Mathieu know, he who had not been trained in the best schools, had never slept between silk sheets? Another detail struck him too: Madame d'Argenti had, of course, neither lied nor exaggerated when she told him she didn't like children, for today, when she was with Mathieu in some public place and heard the crying of one such minuscule adversary, her face would immediately redden with a strange fire and with her fingers in her ears she would stifle the cries of the child she still carried within her, who never stopped moaning, with this confession: "I'd like to pinch those children, throw them to the bottom of a well, believe me!" Her distress was as deep as it was heartfelt. When Monsieur d'Argenti, for his sins, was a witness to one of these scenes, he would tell his wife:

"Calm down, calm down, you always make too much fuss about everything. Please, my darling, calm yourself."

For Antoine d'Argenti, who adored children, nothing could be more distressing, Mathieu thought, than to have a wife capable of spreading everywhere, even in the blaze of her love, this hatred, this bile. "One can get used to anything though," he told Mathieu. Curiously, Christian and Paul suffered, like their mother, from the same aural phobia. What a peculiar family, he thought. How far he was already from the sabbath peace of his first day in the Parisian gloom! For Mathieu, who before that day had never known that he was as greedy as other men, that he was as voracious and sensual as Madame d'Argenti, life still seemed filled with pleasant times. Madame d'Argenti's soul might change – to her disadvantage – but her body lost none of its luminous attraction for the man who loved her. Mathieu dared not think too much of the other hope that haunted him: his book.

"I've done as I promised, my friend, I've told a critic friend about you; I even mentioned your promising talent."

Mathieu was not too delighted at these words, as "promising" suggested the embryo of what he might become. He wanted "to be," not become, someone. Becoming, promising seemed to him images of nothingness. What was the use, after struggling for twenty years, of being only that, "a state of desire in the belly of the world?" Nevertheless, he smiled complacently at his benefactress.

"Thank you," he said, kissing her hand.

"But why do you thank me? Perhaps you'll be successful. One hears so much about your country these days. Almost too much, I might say. Quebec this, Quebec that – you really take up too much room. And yet it's not even a large country."

Mathieu knew that Madame d'Argenti was highly cultivated and intelligent, so he excused her ignorance of geographical proportions, for to her Mathieu's country was smaller than Brittany. Still nurtured by the prejudices of Voltaire, she saw no reason to change her way of thinking. Would France change hers? No. What was admirable about Mathieu Lelièvre's newly adopted country, she declared, was the nineteenth century and its faded poetry. Did Mathieu, son of the steppes violated by the dauntlessness of North American cities, not understand that it was an art for a country to preserve its traditions, not to change? Did he not love the unchanging cathedrals? The rock of tradition? Mathieu acknowledged that Madame d'Argenti was correct to say that people spoke of Quebec a great deal; the hour had struck and Mathieu chimed in along with his country.

Would he not be honoured too, for his truly Québécois freshness and imagination? Would people not say of him "Welcome to this new writer who has come to us from the cold?" Like Madame d'Argenti, he marked off a whole litany of epithets concerning his *oeuvre* with no remorse; he was concupiscent. And every day he spent a little more money. Monsieur d'Argenti, though he spent less, was weighed down by debts.

"Think of it, my friend, I've put a great deal of money into that property in Normandy. It was for Yvonne; she coveted it at any price, but she's no happier there, so what can I do? She doesn't enjoy the country, she says, but is that any reason to ruin me? And yet I've done everything to adorn that rustic sadness, I've bought velvet curtains, a sofa . . . but she keeps telling me it's funereal as a church. Now she wants an estate in Ireland and several *hectares* in Portugal. Who do you think could buy her that? She dreams of the sea, of grass that's always green. She's insatiable, as I've told you! But you mustn't judge her too harshly, my friend, she's improving: one day we learned from the newspapers – alas! my friend, one should never read the papers – that India was in the grip of famine. Well, Yvonne immediately had a notion of going to help those unfortunate victims, of going there . . . Is that not generous? Of course I explained that it wouldn't be very wise and she understood. Could she tolerate the life there? With those wretched people who don't even belong to her race? No, she's far too fragile! Too gracious for the misfortunes of this world that overwhelm us all! Believe me, she is truly good, but she often hides it, out of modesty. Ah, the mystery of human beings, my friend, the mystery!"

Monsieur d'Argenti broke off his monologue to lose himself in a long reflection, and Mathieu understood that when his friend began to think it was within an inner darkness, he extinguished any light from the outside and saw no one, particularly not Mathieu Lelièvre, who sat facing him; Mathieu was still lulled by the musical voice that had spoken to him of Madame d'Argenti and he wondered if Monsieur d'Argenti's portrait of his wife was not painted with too lenient a brush. Mathieu recalled that one evening he had gone with Madame d'Argenti to visit her illustrious friend Madame Colombe (the very name set him dreaming), author of an admirably pornographic novel he had read when he was fourteen. He had been disappointed that he could not experience all the adventures the oracle of eroticism offered him simply with words and he recalled a conversation between Madame d'Argenti and the famous author that still made him shudder with uncertainty, perhaps because he had been ashamed and did not admit it until later. Madame Colombe herself had exclaimed as she cut her *escalope de veau:* "The problem of India, *ma chère,* can only be resolved by an atomic bomb and that's what we should wish for those poor people. Believe me, they're lazy and vile enough to deserve it."

To Mathieu's great surprise this declaration did not have the power to take Madame d'Argenti's breath away; on the contrary, she sighed with relief. "You're so right, my friend; that's exactly what I think."

Was this the same woman who "wanted to go to India to rescue the unfortunate" as her husband had said? Perhaps Mathieu was dreaming, or his hearing was deteriorating. And yet, Madame Colombe was a respectable woman and for a long time she had represented for Mathieu, when he was still in short pants, Woman. Was he confusing the writer and her work, those spiritual twins that are so often, as experience now proved to him, physical antitheses? Today he was listening to this eminence of knowledge – and of pleasure too, perhaps, though he had some doubts where that was concerned – announce to a Parisian table surrounded by eager listeners that a people's salvation lay in a bloodbath, and he couldn't believe it. However, neither Madame d'Argenti nor Madame Colombe asked him what he thought of these atrocities, and the suppressed cry that shuddered in his throat did not reach the women, for they were speaking among themselves with no concern for him and he felt it useless to want to cut with his own harsh sounds the rock of their united bigotry.

He learned later that Madame Colombe was called Madame Bourroux, but the author had deemed it easier to conceal her sex beneath the plumage of a bird; and the dove in its honourable flight might well act as a shield against the arrows of censorship. What surprised Mathieu as well was that while Madame d'Argenti was reverential towards Madame Colombe when she saw her, she was much less so towards Madame Bourroux when she did not. "Ah! that woman is so hardhearted, so miserly!" she would say; "I've been seeing her for fifteen years now and believe me, she's never given me a thing, though she's a millionaire. Shocking, isn't it? One has an obligation to give when one is rich. She hides all her valuable pictures, who knows where – under the mattress? inside the walls? You saw her, she even hesitated over the tip, saying she didn't have a centime. Ah! there's nothing more dangerous than a whore disguised as a nun, believe me!"

But if she saw Madame Colombe the following day she would suddenly become all concerned. "Ah! my poor friend, are you suffering? You had indigestion? How you suffer! You mustn't go out tomorrow, I'll bring you a few slices of ham; my poor friend, who in this world suffers as you do?"

Dazed, Mathieu Lelièvre, like Antoine d'Argenti before him, became accustomed to Madame d'Argenti's numerous metamorphoses. It was no doubt out of novelistic zeal (for, as Mathieu told himself, what can stop a writer from inventing even his own life, from continuing the story when it ends) that Madame d'Argenti said of her friend: "When I think that at thirteen she slept with her father, and at forty with her son; that woman has done everything, take my word for it! And now, my friend, let me ask you something: Why not? I envy her! Particularly in this case; it's rewarded me enormously. If the simple act of sleeping with someone could make us rich I'd be a millionaire many times over today myself!"

Mathieu, who experienced all his novels at once and no longer knew which one was closer to the truth, searched Madame Colombe's face for a trace of incestuous creases lost in time. But he saw nothing, as he had before him only a personage inhabited by her own *oeuvre*, who looked like a soberly dressed schoolteacher pulling her sweater around her and frowning behind her eyeglasses as she read the menu; no, this woman, so Catholic in appearance, could not be the one who, according to Madame d'Argenti's literary interpretation, "once prostituted herself simply for pleasure in some distinguished places; you know we have special restaurants for that sort of recreation." Once again Madame d'Argenti was living her *oeuvre*. Such a crowning achievement of eroticism could not end like this, in a stocky body on which nature had inflicted such drab complaints as constipation, migraines and indigestion; these illnesses most likely belonged to Madame Bourroux, the other, sister of everyday life, prisoner of a frenzied mind. However, Mathieu hoped to meet in the person of Madame Colombe's son, Oedipus himself. But the son, despite his sumptuous incest, was crowned with no tragedy; he was a bald young man so timid that he blushed, who had mistresses and seemed to demonstrate none of the signs of a creature predestined to a dark fate. And if it was true that Madame Colombe the writer was a millionaire, why did she deprive Madame Bourroux, the woman, of meat, saying "it's too expensive"?

"Ah! niggardly as she is, she won't leave me anything in her will, but I still go to see her assiduously! And do you know why, my friend? Because I'm good . . . that's why!"

What could he do, Mathieu wondered, but let himself be convinced and permeated by all of Madame d'Argenti's emanations? She alone knew just how good she really was. Was it not a masterful expression of this feeling to invite Mathieu Lelièvre for cocktails at the Academy? Mathieu told himself that eventually he would be noticed in these cultural sanctuaries, but weeks passed and he still went unremarked. His novel had just been born, silently, without tears, like many children of silence. Nor was his person noticed either, even at the gracious side of Madame d'Argenti, sipping a drink, his expression langourous, trying to entice some of the Parisian intellectuals prowling about the buffet like wild beasts around a scene of slaughter. In the midst of this hungry competition Mathieu no longer existed. Madame d'Argenti herself devoured a sandwich that she held in her fingertips: she didn't eat, Mathieu thought, no, with her swimmer's pink cheeks, her ethereal manner, she "tasted." Tender now, Mathieu thought of the beautiful things he would say about his mistress to her husband that evening. But Antoine received Mathieu Lelièvre with an unusual detachment that was not habitual, saying: "Of course, my friend, the woman is very charming, but I'm tired of paying all her bills. I'm going to Tunisia." And asking Paul to pack his bags, Antoine left at dawn, saying goodbye for a few days to "all these carryings-on that keep me from sleeping," as he muttered angrily. And so Mathieu had time to study the first reviews that greeted his book: "If there were a prize for bad books young Mathieu Lelièvre would win it"; they said, too, that the author's work was bereft of "Québécois qualities" and, finally, who was this imitator of Rousseau who wrote his Memoirs as he stood on the threshold of life? No, Mathieu Lelièvre was not "a writer from the cold" but "a writer who was party to the lukewarm society life of Paris" – and Paris already had too many authors of that sort! Ah! thought Mathieu, wounded, what balm could heal his wounds? While he waited, Pierre-Henri Lajeunesse sent him every week, meticulously clipping them with the enemy's scissors, newspaper articles from his own country, and Mathieu regularly slaked his thirst with the arsenic of these testimonials from those he still called in his letters "his friends, his colleagues." "This is a hare that should have stayed in its burrow," they said, or "Mathieu Lelièvre isn't one of us, he's French." All the same, Mathieu was delighted because at last, people were talking about him. He dreamed of his readers, those who read "bad books," for, he told himself, who would be mad enough to read a masterpiece? But he wasn't so humble as to believe that he hadn't written one himself, in his way. Who until now had been original enough to date his Memoirs from the first day of his life? If his first work didn't shatter the literary world with the fortissimo sound of an orchestra, it would learn, little by little, that Mathieu Lelièvre was a voice in the chorus, a feeble gnashing of teeth or − who knows − a murmur. But while he yielded to the emotion of having this small, completed life run away from him, Madame d'Argenti grew morose. It was as though the independent existence Mathieu dragged everywhere with him, to dinner with friends of Madame d'Argenti or on their solitary walks in the country, was beginning to irritate her. She told Mathieu he was "too fond of himself, and of his book," she added jealously; at more serious moments she said she had been "disappointed." Mathieu no longer knew what to give her, for with a weary hand she would brush away any compliment, saying: "No, I want nothing more, I've been too sorely wounded." But was she wounded because she believed that people were talking about Mathieu Lelièvre too much in the newspapers or because the voluptuous tide of attention of which her lover no longer received merely kindly drops was withdrawing from her?

"The only thing that would really please me, my friend − but what's the use, you can't give it to me − would be a trip to London."

"Why not?"

"And my debts? And the bills from Saint-Laurent?" Madame d'Argenti exclaimed. "I'm so unlucky! When Antoine went away he wasn't even considerate enough to relieve me of these concerns. But you, my friend, you're not like him, I can sense that you love me more than my debts."

"And in London, could I meet your daughter?"

"What daughter? Do I have a daughter?" Madame d'Argenti replied curtly.

"Didn't you tell me she was studying in London? You know very well that anything close to you interests me."

Even if Mathieu Lelièvre attempted with these words to express the conqueror's tender possessiveness, breathing into his "anything that is close to you" a sort of literary punctuation, Madame d'Argenti was not touched, for she dismissed this intruder who reminded her, indiscreetly, that she had given birth "without even wanting them, not only to two helpless sons, which is miserable enough, but to a noxious daughter who's taken my inheritance, my mother's estate, yes! *Mon Dieu,* when will they give me justice," she exclaimed suddenly, beating her breast, and Mathieu remembered too late that Antoine d'Argenti had, in fact, told him of "the hostile relationship between Madame d'Argenti and her daughter, over something to do with an estate."

"How could a mother not love her daughter?" he asked foolishly, for in his embarrassment he didn't know what to say.

"And my own mother, did she love me?" Madame d'Argenti replied, her eyes sparkling with a fire Mathieu had not seen before. "If she loved me why did she tear my bread, my food, my inheritance from my mouth?" she concluded, weeping. "A person who is neglected by her mother in that way is entitled to commit any crime. At least that's what you read in books! What do you have to complain about, my friend? Not only did your mother adore you, your father respects you, which is an injustice; but you were born in a country that has never known either plague or war, you're a child weaned on happiness and good health, that's what you are. Ah, how unhappy I am!"

Mathieu listened attentively: Madame d'Argenti was right, he thought; all privileged people like him were guilty. They left for London and Madame d'Argenti, still in the throes of despondency, scarcely glanced at the large white clouds they passed over during the flight; she set foot on English soil grumbling that she'd had "a very bad journey, and you know why, my friend, because all I saw in the airplane was you and your hair. You blocked out the entire landscape with that hair that comes right down to your collar. Why must you wear it so long? Do I have that much hair? No, and yet I'm attractive all the same!"

Mathieu listened with amazement to this remark, for Madame d'Argenti was not accustomed to observe anyone but herself. Why was she suddenly talking to him about his hair? Was it a sign that he was beginning to have an external existence for her, or was it the opposite – the reflection of love grown cold, objective to the point of intolerance? If today she took offence at the disproportion of Mathieu Lelièvre's head (and the unseemliness of his hair), what would she say tomorrow about his feet? Mathieu wanted to explain that his was like all the other abundantly hairy heads in his country, but if he spoke of that abundance would he not evoke for her, already jealous of his privileged life, all the other forms of wealth and fertility of which she felt deprived?

"They might very well not allow us in the Hôtel Georges V because of you."

Mathieu didn't dare say he had hoped to take Madame d'Argenti to a bed-and-breakfast; it would have been too distressing to her, with her taste for luxury, but when she ordered a lobster for dinner he grew dizzy.

"But Yvonne, what will become of us when we have no more money?"

"We'll leave each other, my friend, we'll leave each other." Her ability to speak in such a detached manner, in such a casual voice, all the while listening to Mathieu's champagne glass clink against her own, about what frightened him so much – the end of their affair – an omen he knew now might become reality – shook Mathieu out of his dream. He who had known only in his thoughts the fear of displeasing Madame d'Argenti, sometimes not breathing at night so she might abandon herself quite freely to her gentle snoring, he who had tormented his mind with this fear, now displeased her – and doing so caused him less pain than the fear that it might happen. Madame d'Argenti did not understand that she no longer had before her the Mathieu Lelièvre she had known so well, but, suddenly, a tragic hero, the sort one finds in all love stories; but since this story was not hers she kept looking at her lover with the same smile, a smile he knew well too, that did not change because Mathieu was suffering, and she said to him as she had said the night before:

"Eat, my friend, you must eat to live."

But for Mathieu, emerging from his dream, finding himself so soon at the end of a novel he had imagined would be longer than life, eating and living now meant nothing.

He stared at Madame d'Argenti, into her eyes, and his expression seemed to say: "You have just sentenced me to death," but happily for her, Madame d'Argenti felt icily indifferent to this sort of language. As for Mathieu, he thought of the sleepless nights he must face as he repeated, with the hope that he would never have to convince himself of it: "She doesn't love me any more" or, if he wanted to make his torture more piquant: "Has she ever loved me?" He could not believe in such a wretched fate, he who had been so happy a few days earlier when he went to meet Madame d'Argenti at the door of a shop or in the intimacy of one of those Parisian evenings before the feverish dinner hour, when he fastened about her neck the gold chain she had coveted and which she now cared nothing about, for all the time she had been smiling at him, dreamy but not thinking of him, running her fingers through the precious ornament around her neck, pulling on the chain of love that had made her a prisoner, and Mathieu Lelièvre thought as he watched her scratch at the flimsy rings: "Ah! each of these links is a drop of my blood" while, at the same time, Madame d'Argenti was wondering why Mathieu had suddenly assumed "that rather foolish expression," not even recognizing that the face she didn't understand was the face of disappointed passion.

"What's wrong with you this evening, my friend?" she asked impatiently. "Have you given a thought to the difficult day I must face tomorrow? Think of it, I must see the daughter I loathe. It's torture! She's formidable, you'll see. I ask you, what is more monstrous than our children? You're no doubt thinking about the child of yours that's come between us – your book."

But Mathieu was so sad he thought that never again would he be capable of writing a single line. "What's the use? All is dead . . . " drifted through his mind like a white banner of surrender; he would never read books again, he would never sleep again, he might as well bid life farewell. Then he began to realize that if Madame d'Argenti represented beauty, he himself was intelligence, and this filled him with pride, for intelligence meant a faculty for suffering, while beauty's was to impose suffering through all sorts of wiles. Thus, without knowing it, Mathieu Lelièvre was writing. And in the *oeuvre* he was beginning to imagine, he reproached Madame d'Argenti for her beauty, all the while praising his own good looks – but for more subtle motives. He even came round to thinking that his unhappiness was bearable. The next morning he was astonished to see that life still went on. Madame d'Argenti, who was often cheerful in the morning, sang as she took her bath, as usual. And as she did every day, she touched her small earlobes with a few drops of perfume. Then she took over the telephone, authoritatively arranging a meeting with her daughter at a café in the City. "She's formidable, you'll see; I tremble in her presence," she told Mathieu again. But he no longer even hoped that by growing closer to Madame d'Argenti's daughter he might conquer the mother once again. However, despite his extreme sorrow he was delighted when he saw a discreet young girl approach them, who was not only not "formidable" but was as gentle as her mother was harsh, so that when he caught a glimpse of the girl he could dream again of the one he had lost; for Madame d'Argenti was, he thought, simply the other side of this gentleness: wrath. That morning especially, Madame d'Argenti represented the summit of such wrath and she pushed away the daughter who was coming towards her to embrace her, exclaiming:

"Ah! you perfidious creature, you've ruined me! Don't kiss me!" Berthe, intimidated, murmured in English: "Good morning," then seeing that her mother was hungry, expressed, in French, the desire to share an English cake with her.

"What, have you forgotten your mother tongue? How could you forget me, your own mother? I know very well that I've confined you here in England since your childhood, but was it my fault? There are no bonds between us, young lady; I didn't love you, you had a way of crying in your cradle that I didn't like at all. Ah! what could I do, these things happen. I thought that rather than give in to a criminal urge — and believe me, the desire was strong — it would be better to send her across the Channel. And for that your grandmother accused me of being an inhuman mother and passed on to you who were only a baby, a mere foetus, all my inheritance! But was it not more humane to put you out of my sight? Ah! I was all too human where you were concerned, and now you speak to me in a language I despise!"

"How's Antoine?" Berthe asked respectfully.

"Antoine? How can you speak of your father that way? Antoine my husband? Your father has nothing now, nothing, he begs me to borrow a little money from you. It's Christian and the other one, the failure, Paul — in any case, quite frankly, they're both failures — your brothers are slowly killing your father. He's pale and so unhappy he's in Tunisia now, resting . . . with some boy who won't waste any time before he robs him . . . Because in those countries one can expect anything . . . And your father never changes."

Mathieu Lelièvre could tell himself: "Ah, how cruel Madame d'Argenti is, with her pitiless heart," while at the same moment she surprised him with one of those abrupt changes of mood of which she herself was the first victim, for, still carried away by the leaps of her disposition, she seemed to have forgotten she had told her daughter: "Get away from me, you whom I do not love," borrowing from Racine the tone of religious fervour she admired in literature as in life, when she added, pleading, a few minutes later: "Poor little Berthe, you need a coat, let me buy you one."

Although these two jolts came from the same creature they were no longer part of her as she looked at her daughter with her rather glaucous eyes and asked, as though to reassure herself: "What's wrong with you, child? Will you refuse me the pleasure of offering you a gift?"

Suddenly plunged into the fascination of doubt (was Madame d'Argenti evil or too generous, etc.?) with respect to Berthe, who was silently observing her mother, Mathieu regretted that he had given in too soon to the temptation of judging Madame d'Argenti more according to her actions than her thoughts, for as he told himself again, who knows, even an evil act may sometimes conceal a noble thought. Madame d'Argenti seemed to love her daugher in her fashion, and as she was fond of saying: "My fashion of loving resembles only myself," a statement that should have incited Mathieu to more clemency.

"Berthe, my angel, you know I'm irritable so why must you irritate me? You read the *London News* now? What can you understand of that atrocious language? I have an ear only for the French of Paris."

And it was true that this language, the French of Paris, sometimes flowed from Madame d'Argenti's lips like a liqueur: she was a huntress who tracked down any accent from Marseille or the Auvergne, she could sniff in the distance any grammar too lilting, any syllable too coarse. Madame d'Argenti heard only her own music: if she recited poems in a clear and pious voice or spoke of religion to her husband, this liqueur that moistened her lips would immediately inundate the soul of Mathieu Lelièvre and intoxicate it with so many mellow sounds. Mathieu knew, however, that Madame d'Argenti was not so melodramatic every day, that piercing cries often ran through the crystal of her speech, of the sort one sometimes hears in a barnyard; but he thought that after their love was dead he would still hear within him, cooing, this voice of an unchanging culture, for he told himself that while a woman may deceive you and wither, culture is preserved forever.

After begging a little affection from her daughter while stroking her cheek with her own delicate hand, Madame d'Argenti said suddenly to Mathieu: "And you, do you still love me as much as ever? Of course I know very well that no one has ever loved me as you do," she answered, not waiting for Mathieu's reply. "Very well, since we're all so happy, the three of us, we shall go to the theatre this evening. Berthe, do you know of a French theatre in this city of barbaric noises?"

Mathieu was astonished that Madame d'Argenti, who was so fond of the question "Do you love me?" was so seldom generous with the declaration "I love you." It was as though she had never dreamed of uttering these three brief words, not because of hardness but from a sense of economy that feared, through this confession, losing its identity. Or else perhaps it was out of laziness that she avoided saying what it cost her so little to hear. But, Mathieu thought, if Madame d'Argenti was a writer, why did she have so little concern for human life? She reflected a great deal, and a solemn line would suddenly cast a shadow over her fine forehead. She often took her notebooks and pencils to bed, but when did she direct her gaze, like the light of a lamp, outside her books and towards the inferno below, where most people struggled? The sky she contemplated from the solitude of her sheets as she bit on her pencil was empty of all those demons with which Mathieu Lelièvre's mind was overflowing. As she sat there in the midst of her white corolla, was she not the very expression of opaque thought, obscure and inaccessible? Mathieu promised himself to show these new portraits of the writer to Antoine d'Argenti as soon as he returned, but Antoine came back from Tunisia with such a youthful air that Mathieu felt it incongruous to raise such serious matters so soon. Antoine had met Ashmed in the alleys of Tunis. "Just imagine," he told Mathieu, happy that

68

he could, through his account, evoke the beloved face, "they were going to put the poor child in prison . . . And why? Some story about prostitution with tourists! That angel prostitute himself? I saved him, naturally, I took him to the mountains with me. Look at this photograph – such a friendly face, don't you think? I know Yvonne will be very hostile to the idea, but I intend to go back and fetch him and invite him home. He could study in Paris like one of my sons. It was very hot and he wore patched blue jeans – nothing underneath, no underwear, ah! You'll see, he's an adorable child."

Mathieu listened to Antoine d'Argenti like an exile hearing descriptions of heavenly lands, for Antoine talked about his loves so well that often one had only to listen to him in order to share the pleasure of loving. Mathieu thought as he watched Monsieur d'Argenti, his hands curved majestically, describe little Ashmed's sleeping body, that when the man spoke of his own life he had the same powers of evocation as good books: seduced by his verbal grandeur, Mathieu became in turn each of the characters in the account he was hearing. He was Antoine d'Argenti walking through the sunny streets of Tunis in his linen suit, straw hat elegantly tilted forward, and Ashmed with hot bare thighs running through the dust as the policemen chased him. When Monsieur d'Argenti completed his touching memories by evoking "the child's scarred brown cheek . . . A knife wound he got when he was five, but he's tender-hearted, you'll see . . . " Mathieu touched his own cheek as a sign of compassion.

"I had the pleasure of meeting your daughter in London," he said suddenly, ashamed he had already forgotten Berthe.

"My daughter? Ah yes, charming, quite charming . . . " said Antoine, succumbing to the other charm he carried inside him. "Alas, he added dreamily, "Yvonne doesn't care for her."

"Madame d'Argenti even told her daughter, in my presence," said Mathieu, suddenly forgetting all discretion and taking advantage of the confidential atmosphere that surrounded him, "yes, that one day, long ago, she had even wanted to kill Berthe in her cradle."

"Ah!" said Antoine, suddenly irritated at this display of naiveté, for why must Mathieu Lelièvre speak to him yet again of his wife, particularly at this moment? "Ah!" he exclaimed, getting up from his chair, "don't you realize that's what is called exaggeration? An exaggeration of guilt, yes, and as I've already told you, guilt distorts people! Besides," he added more calmly, "the story about Berthe's cradle isn't true, it's from a novel. If all my wife's novels were like life, where would we be now? Would you and I still be real? And if it were true that in an impetuous moment my wife shook our daughter's cradle a little roughly, did Berthe die from it, yes or no? Her English lycée costs me dearly – it's too much, I tell you, one must pity an exhausted mother who's nervous too, very nervous. As you know, my wife is very fragile . . . "

Mathieu Lelièvre thought that Monsieur d'Argenti's knowledge of his wife and of the writer in her was narrower than his own, though he was only passing through their lives. However, had he not read in another of Madame d'Argenti's novels a sinister passage in which, a few days after its birth, a mother throws a child from her lap to the marble floor, in the silence of some suburban hospital? Had he dreamed this scene or was it Madame d'Argenti who had related Paul's difficult birth? "And he's so happy to be alive today. Look at him, the great lump! Does he have a fractured skull? No, he's simply illiterate, which is more shocking." Where was reality and where did fabrication begin in Madame d'Argenti's books as in her daily life? As each person wrote out his life to the rhythm of his worst dreams, did he not risk uncovering in the depth of his being a strangler of children here, there a sleeping hangman only waiting for the occasion to punish weak flesh, what Madame d'Argenti called in her books – describing children – "embryonic flesh"? Mathieu loved Madame d'Argenti too much to hear beneath her rippling laughter anything but the laughter of innocence: if she was the fiery criminal of her own writing, how could she be such a master of all the yearnings for repentance? Human crimes are discreet so it was curious, Mathieu thought, that in literature people were capable of acting so noisily. For he seemed to hear the baby fall onto the marble floor, to catch as well the horrified whispers in the room; he was on the point of sharing this observation with Monsieur d'Argenti when the latter said to him abruptly:

"Fine, we've talked enough about that, Etienne will be here in a few moments and you know I must dismiss you, for my appointments with Etienne are strictly private."

Mathieu did not immediately understand that the door was being opened for him onto the cold street; he stayed where he was, his heavy shoes anchored in the d'Argentis' green carpet. He saw Etienne walk past him without shaking his hand and go to Antoine who was waiting in his room. He remembered then that Monsieur d'Argenti had told him that Etienne – what a disappointment, a brilliant boy – had just left his studies to become "an antique dealer, now tell me, is that an occupation for a boy like him?" As he listened to the hum of conversation between the two friends Mathieu knew that Etienne had a greater gift for trade than for art, for he was saying: "It's a fake fifteenth-century table, but I got a very nice price from the woman I sold it to."

"Fake, you say, my friend? Ah!" Antoine d'Argenti replied wearily, "my dear Etienne, what is false . . . what is true . . . Nowadays, what difference is there?"

Mathieu told himself that the anomaly was not within them but within himself; he had a moral code while they did not: do not lie, do not steal – why should these prohibitions affect him more than they did Antoine and Etienne? Was it because he was not yet a divinity in his own eyes? For if he too had experienced that delight, would he suddenly become like them? A man without scruples perhaps, but kind to himself. "A fake antique table," he said to himself, "why

71

not? Etienne is right – how can you tell what is false when you're paying for it? It's all there, in the paradox of truth – and truth is everywhere, isn't it?" If Monsieur d'Argenti had a slight tendency to lie, and Etienne to steal, and if Madame d'Argenti had other mysterious kinds of infamous behaviour, who but they themselves could pass judgement on their acts in all their quiet ambiguity? Did Monsieur d'Argenti not say of himself that he was "a saviour of souls?" That he had "a pleasant nature" and that he was always "even-tempered"? And did Madame d'Argenti not say with sighs of exaltation that she sometimes "approached saintliness?" Meanwhile, Antoine would show a photograph of Ashmed to Etienne, who said in the voice of a connoisseur: "Another little savage I'd like to break in for you, Antoine, but you like them too young."

"I'll bring him to Paris, here to my family. Of course I must speak to Yvonne about it first," said Monsieur d'Argenti. "I know, I could suggest she spend her winter vacation in Tunisia; that would be a way to win her over to the child . . . Yes, why not? I'll speak to Mathieu about it, because she needs distractions . . . yes, and she needs someone with her . . . I'll mention it to her when she comes back from her evening with Madame Colombe."

Mathieu had often dreamed of travelling with Madame d'Argenti but now he considered gloomily that the most beautiful journeys are ill-suited to the death pangs of love. Why go away if it is only to find the same pain everywhere? Madame d'Argenti asked, "How can you give the name pain to something that is only chronic languour?" for although she did not love Mathieu Lelièvre and freely admitted that she had never loved him, she could not understand why he should have stopped loving her.

"In any event, what are you complaining about? Don't we sleep together like good friends? And since I don't love you, why should I not have the right to deceive you? I reproach you for nothing, my friend; do you think I scorn your freshness, your tenderness, the gifts that flow constantly from the fountain of your childish heart? Do you underestimate me that much? Ah! my dear, you cause me great sorrow!"

The deeper Mathieu Lelièvre buried himself in sorrow, the more playful Madame d'Argenti became, throwing herself into preparations for their summer in Tunis, dragging Mathieu into more expenses, more extravagances which, she said, would revive his spirits. Mathieu did not know how poor he was, but he observed with pleasure that his book "seemed to be selling," if invisibly, for in the past few days he had not seen it in bookstore windows; no, from the outside, where for several weeks the book had sparkled like a sun during its minuscule existence, the book that had been so protected and so cherished – and its author too – had just crossed the threshold of retirement. "But don't worry about such a small matter," said Madame d'Argenti, reassuring Mathieu with a penetrating look; "what isn't seen sells better . . . I've already told you, my friend, you and I are too good to be bestsellers. Let's go to Hermès, I've just seen the most divine tennis outfit there and for you, some absolutely ravishing shorts. Ah! we'll be so happy there, my friend!" And who knows, Mathieu thought, as he signed his last traveller's cheques, carrying the white shorts under his arm, who could prove that Madame d'Argenti was wrong, for perhaps it was true, as she said, that "a book in a shop isn't necessarily dead; look at mine – they still sell, but one never sees them! Great writers are never famous, you and I know that!"

But Mathieu Lelièvre was even more surprised to find himself travelling without even seeing or feeling. It was probably because Madame d'Argenti was always there, in the same room, the same bed, using the same perfume, slipping her foot into the same shoe every morning, most likely because one's habits resist even changes in geography. To Mathieu, Tunis resembled London and London, Tunis. He wondered whether his affair with Madame d'Argenti might not become, in such a place, a shade less gloomy thanks to Ashmed and Monsieur d'Argenti who loved each other until it turned them pale, while he and Madame d'Argenti became brown without loving. Even though Madame d'Argenti wanted to make love at four in the morning so she could get up early "to take the sun before lunch when it's too hot," Mathieu found in her desire no encouragement to passion, for he was more inclined to sleep at that hour, having been kept awake for long periods all night long by the morose agitation of his thoughts and the stormy presence of the wind on his face. Even though the nights were cool, Madame d'Argenti liked to sleep naked, with the window open, "abandoned to the fury of all the elements, particularly in this foreign land," she said, so that Mathieu felt as though they were sleeping in a hammock shaken by the sea winds. Beneath his rather wan suntan Mathieu shivered, telling himself he would soon fall sick, which seemed to resolve everything, for it would be better to be sick than deceived by the blandness of the days (but was it not he in fact who was so deceiving himself?). One could truly say that Madame d'Argenti was deceiving him, even if it was only in thought, for she was flourishing, golden, loving even to the sick person, as she soothed Mathieu's shivering with velvety perfumed caresses, for she had got in the habit of eating from her basket of fruit in bed at dawn, and her kisses, the balm of her fruity digestion, always invaded Mathieu like the perfumes from a garden. When he didn't find himself lying on a bunch of grapes, he would awaken with his hair full of orange peels that Madame d'Argenti had thrown onto him rather than out on the balcony where her bathing suit lay limp on the railing, the two pieces so brief they looked like swaddling bands, sentimentally fragile objects that would have moved Mathieu early in his encounter with her but now, as time drew on, the money dwindled and so did love, intensifying the beating of his heart. What would become of him when he returned to Paris? Would he leave Madame d'Argenti, would he finally have the courage to do so? Was his future not like the violet sky of the Tunisian dawn – assassinated? "Ah!" he wondered, "where are the French people I once dreamed of?" Not in Paris, in the d'Argentis' circle, nor in the sumptuous hotel where at breakfast time Mathieu found, in other forms, the faces of Antoine and Etienne, the same invocations and almost the same sighs as in Paris, travelling as germs do, and birds. Mathieu fell into the disenchantment that follows ecstasy: now that he was no longer happy with Madame d'Argenti, he was better able to struggle against her charm; at the same time however, he grew sad when he got up in the morning without the anticipation of exciting surprises that would fill his hours. Madame d'Argenti no longer surprised him and that seemed catastrophic. He even began – as she had done several weeks earlier – to observe some of her defects, and nothing seemed so pitiless to him as the countenance that for a long time had seen nothing, known nothing, but that suddenly – like the blade of disillusionment cutting through dreams – brings very close, in every crude detail, everything that yesterday, in the distance, was so beautiful. Yesterday, he had found Madame d'Argenti's appetite admirable, today he thought she ate too much. When she came in from swimming or from a long sweltering siesta on the hotel terrace, one might have said that she resembled all the vacationers who, despite the golden flesh outside their bathing suits, came from a starving Europe in decline, and she too attacked, with teeth and mouth and hand, all the pleasures of the table. The servants, upright in their rigid dignity, a distant smile on their lips, watched the flock of foreigners as they decimated – with no regard for them – the displays of their wealth; here they tore off pieces of roasted kid that had cooked while Madame d'Argenti was baking in the sun, preparing to eat it; around it spread the aroma of its sacrifice but, as she said to Mathieu, "it's not the time to be thinking about that"; while there, on silver plates, large pink bloody fish still milled about. "Ah! it's all too good," said Madame d'Argenti. "One mustn't choose, my friend, one must take everything. Why do you hesitate, that's why it's there; take two carafes of wine as well, it costs the same in any event." What troubled Mathieu most, Madame d'Argenti seemed prepared to wolf down such a feast three times a day. Although Monsieur d'Argenti ate just as much, he never lost his appearance of temperamental refinement; while Madame d'Argenti would undulate in the sand, like someone making love, Mathieu thought, her bronzed thigh a little broader every day, Antoine had never been so long and slender as in his Tunisian tunic and there was, in his condescension of one who looks down from above, an almost priestly aspect. Mathieu would meet him during the hours of coolness, walking by the sea, one hand on Ashmed's shoulder, guiding the one he called his "little shepherd"; but in the brief orange pants Monsieur d'Argenti, with jealous care, had bought him in Paris (but which Ashmed didn't like "because that's for a girl, not for Ashmed"), the shepherd, whom Monsieur d'Argenti would have liked to keep at his side forever peaceful, was vivacious as a trout and he sprang and leaped like a young tiger. Frequently, to console himself, Monsieur d'Argenti − melancholy, perhaps, but always noble − would look towards the group of adolescent fishermen who were, with shouts of joy, pushing their small twilit craft to shore. The frolicking of all these bony bodies, the glowing fire of all the little faces around their boat, formed a scene that every evening plunged Monsieur d'Argenti into smiling meditation. "Such charming creatures on this earth," he seemed to be thinking as his feet and the bottom of his tunic rested in the water; "why must we always love only one?" "You have cigarette, Monsieur? Cigarette for Ashmed?" for all the children whom Monsieur d'Argenti met were called Ashmed; the thin voice came to him with the first, much hoped-for breeze. "Cigarette, just one cigarette for Ashmed," and barely turning around so he would lose none of the evening moisture or the music of the waves at his feet, Monsieur d'Argenti dispensed from the tips of his fingers at the end of an arm stretched out like a tree, its fruits – the miraculous cigarettes. While the chorus enveloped him in gratitude and one of their faces invited him to hope, "What velvet in those eyes, what rough sympathy in the clasp of his hand," he thought, he could not forget Ashmed's flight to his former life, for if he lost sight for one moment of his "street sparrow" he would find him on the knees of a German architect in the shadows of the hotel bar, melting with tenderness and sealing with his round-faced kiss some nocturnal agreement, at the same time seizing with his child's hand, long accustomed to excessive professional zeal, his future lover's wallet or watch or tie-pin, but without disturbing in the least, with his wheedling behaviour, his partner's drowsiness. "I'll make him shed that habit in Paris," Monsieur d'Argenti told Mathieu, as though Paris were the city of innocence; but beginning today he inflicted a mild punishment on Ashmed, forbidding him to go out at siesta time, for example, for that hour was the most "dangerous" for Monsieur d'Argenti. Ashmed, wide awake while others dozed, would slip into bedrooms that had the white intimacy of cells. In them, while he played, as he told Monsieur d'Argenti later, he prayed a little. No one could know the taste of repentance as Ashmed would if he were deprived of his freedom: tears would well up like a flood of pearls on his cheeks; he would prostrate himself at Monsieur d'Argenti's knees: at his feet, he would fall into such sobbing convulsions that Monsieur d'Argenti, as loving as he was horrified, would allow his penitent to flee, knowing full well that an hour later he would find him in the arms of a man or woman who would promise him – "for just one kiss" – "a trip to Nice, a stroll through Tangiers." Ashmed also passionately adored the city's calèches in which – for the same kiss, the same mischievous wink followed by a stride towards a vacationing millionaire – "Monsieur had a big tip for Ashmed in his pocket." Antoine d'Argenti was driven to despair by all the treasures Ashmed brought to his room in the evening, not only because of jealousy that was legitimate in the circumstances, but also because, like Mathieu Lelièvre with Madame d'Argenti, he would have liked to be the only person able to discharge all his resources on his protégé.

"When I think that I deprive my own children for the sake of this little one," he told Mathieu that evening, drinking a martini as the sun sank into the shadowy sea. "I ask you, what more does he want of me? Why must he go to others when I already give him everything? Obviously it's a mystery I can't comprehend . . . For example, those lovely orange shorts I bought for him at Lanvin – well, they're already worn out . . . What can I do? I so enjoy dressing him like a prince."

For Ashmed, who had spent his whole life virtually naked, the regal get-up he put on every morning before devouring his six croissants at Monsieur d'Argenti's side – although Antoine was most patient at teaching him "how to eat with good manners, like a little Frenchman" – this luxuriously Parisian envelope hung on him like a prisoner's robe; he, whose dazzling smile, the dark radiance of his skin, were the only bits of finery without vanity, looked, in the grey schoolboy's suit Monsieur d'Argenti had selected for him with infinite scruples, in Paris, like a sad boarder. Ashmed would frequently give away a pair of shoes or a silk *foulard* in exchange for knives, for which he had a passion. The knife was his master, his rite and his only faith, if one were to believe the evidence slashed into his skin like writing in a book. And when Monsieur d'Argenti placed his hand on Ashmed to caress him, he had no time to abandon himself to any sentimental reflections before Ashmed exclaimed quickly, puffing out his chest: "Here Ashmed fought with knife and won . . . Look at my scar." Antoine d'Argenti would shrug sadly at the warrior, already fierce, thinking that such a sense of honour might be a substitute, for Ashmed, for "the virility, which happily is still budding" of the pugnacious boy he would become; but the boy whose body was complete, tomorrow's man, was still far away and in the sensual child whom Monsieur d'Argenti loved today there were still some peaceful effusions of tenderness. It sometimes happened, as though he were under some miraculous spell – particularly after those long meals when he was so sated he was unable to move from his chair – that Ashmed was well-behaved for a while, his round feverish eyes wandering in their sockets; but it was not very reassuring for Antoine d'Argenti to read all the dreams, the frank declarations that sparkled in those eyes, one of the dreams being the wild desire – for that afternoon Ashmed had just acquired a new pocket-knife – to tease Madame d'Argenti's fleshy arm with the blade as she reached across the table to pluck a piece of fruit. Even though Antoine had frequently said in private that it was "Ashmed's duty to respect Madame d'Argenti."

"I love you but Ashmed not love her."

"Why, my dear? Why don't you love her? She's my wife, she's nice. And she's nice because she's my wife, do you understand?"

"Yes, but even though she's your wife Ashmed not love her. She not nice."

"No, believe me, she's quite perfect and you should love her."

"Ashmed not love her, she say Ashmed 'Dirty little brat, don't drink from my glass.' "

It is true that ever since vague rumours about cholera had started to circulate through the hotel, Madame d'Argenti talked endlessly to Mathieu of her fears.

"Listen, my friend," she said, "I do want to pretend I'm sharing the child's couscous, just to please my husband and because I'm a good woman, but drink from his glass – I ask you! I already tremble at the thought of all the viruses he must be carrying, right into my husband's bed."

When Antoine d'Argenti announced to his wife that he was bringing Ashmed back to Paris, she dashed into the shower the better to wash away her rage and, with it, the certainty that she had been stricken by disease. Then, calmer, she appeared before Mathieu Lelièvre in a flowered garment, saying: "The proof that I love these people is that I dress like them, look . . . " which made Mathieu think that as she said this other tourists were parading around him, with an exotic charm that suddenly embarrassed him, tourists who had come on the same airplane with them, showing one another the same pieces of cloth, the same colours, in similar bedrooms, and that instead of bringing them closer to their hosts, the game of gaudy concealment marked forever the difference that would always exist between Ashmed's people and the d'Argentis of this world. And yet, it was often more than interest in their own appearance that encouraged them to borrow the colours and costumes, even if only for an evening, of the others. Although Mathieu thought that sympathy should never become an effort, Antoine d'Argenti spoke simply of his "effort at sympathy," of his "desire to communicate with the customs of this adorably childlike people." And he was sincere when he praised the "naive qualities we have lost." Had Antoine lived longer with Ashmed, been invited to share the family's food with him, along with his eight brothers and sisters, his cousins and uncles, eating on the ground like them, receiving like a tribute the brotherhood of rice and chicken that they passed from one hand to the other, had he gradually forgotten the gloss of false gestures, through Ashmed he might have espoused the humility in the hearts of those about him. But Antoine d'Argenti did not spend all his days in such warm intimacy and it was beyond the fog of the Ile Saint-Louis, still in the presence of a woman who for better and for worse had been moulded by civilization and crowned by culture, that he aspired – and aspired alone – to the sunshine that Ashmed's face and the faces of all his people spread over Antoine's life. His dream, as he sometimes told Mathieu, when he left the Bank, was never to be separated from Ashmed and his brothers, to curl up with him in some secret corner of this land he adored and let the end of his existence pass by in intoxicating laziness, close to a garden and a fountain. And while he waited Madame d'Argenti was there, and her husband seemed indispensable to her. Antoine must go with her, their arms around each other's waists, to play tennis, while Mathieu walked behind them with the rackets and balls, watching Madame d'Argenti's pleated skirt flutter in the air that was already heavy though it was only nine in the morning, while beneath the skirt was the entire person who seemed unfamiliar to him now that he had stopped loving her, even when he saw her from the back. At the beginning of their liaison he had thought Madame d'Argenti walked as though she were "exquisitely in a hurry," but now it seemed she had a military gait. At times she would stop suddenly, holding out her wrist to Monsieur d'Argenti who would watch the gulls soar through the sky as she tied her sandal; even when she was bent over that way, turning towards Mathieu the uncertain offering of a smile, he was not sure if he was still attracted by her; but at least he had the pleasure of doubt. When Madame d'Argenti trembled slightly at the thought of pleasing less – or even of displeasing – a ray of concern passed through her eyes; it was the fire of a challenge that carried her away, however, and once again Mathieu Lelièvre thought, "I'm not mistaken, I don't love that woman any more." The air was increasingly suffocating, but Antoine d'Argenti was suddenly imbued with a suppleness that was seraphic (though virulent) as he returned the tennis balls to his wife; they clattered against his racket like dry eggs hatching, while Madame d'Argenti exclaimed: "The day is just beginning, my friend. Please don't overdo it, I'm already perspiring."

"What? Are you complaining over such a small matter? You can go swimming afterwards!"

Monsieur d'Argenti was not accustomed to speak to his wife in this manner; Yvonne d'Argenti herself was always astounded when he addressed her in the tone she herself used, as though a part of her had been stolen from her; but that morning Antoine was exasperated, and following a widespread human inclination he preferred to show to his wife – to someone close to him, rather than others – the irascible side of his nature she was already familiar with and which, if he had shown it to Ashmed, the cause of his irritation, would only have further sharpened the cutting edge of his mood. For Ashmed had once again deceived Antoine d'Argenti. If siesta time was for Ashmed the time for midday temptations, the evening, after dinner, was the time for delectation, for concupiscence, when the tourists had eaten well and Ashmed too, his plump little belly beginning to peep through the stripes of his grape-coloured pullover; an entire chorus of desires began to move towards the bar and Ashmed, like the young Bacchus, whom a few moments earlier Monsieur d'Argenti, seeing him asleep in his chair, had called "the baby who must be put to bed," pounded with a rather unsteady foot (for he had drunk some wine from Monsieur d'Argenti's glass) as the indolent diners walked towards the bar, kingdom of shadows where all is erased, even the wrinkles of bitterness and the fat of abundance. For if these same bodies and faces had been seen in full sunlight, one would have thought the human race was corrupt and predestined to engender only ugliness and malediction; mingled like this, though, effaced in the shadows in a bar where the sky was always close to you – for there was no roof to separate you from it – in the borrowed clothing that served them as personalities, all these human beings covered in gold and embroidery, moving their toes in slippers from a fairytale, were transformed into a celestial or planetary inhabitant, their gaze following the movement of the clouds while all around the sea encircled them with its vast and aimless movement. Each of these people, from America or Europe, suddenly reflected on the meaning of his own existence and saw himself so much in harmony, so deliciously at ease in the great order of the universe as he looked at the sky and those vast inky gulfs called clouds, he told himself he was his own sun, his own moon and sky. Ashmed, who was sensitive to any atmosphere of contentment – for in his philosophy one could take more from happy misery than from sad misery, walked along these Roman galleries contemplating the stars and wondering what was so ecstatic up there, besides the night sky that had so often been his only shelter . . . Then, disappointed by all this mysticism – for even Monsieur d'Argenti was speaking to his wife of "the thirst for an ascetic life in the desert, in the midst of the stars" and she was replying, "Yes, my friend, your life is there, your true life of course, if you take along a few little goatherds . . . " Ashmed bit his lower lip and played with the knife in his pocket, then went to join the bar boys, his own people, those who spoke his language, who laughed like him and – most of all – who offered him "a glass of punch for the boy that nice Monsieur d'Argenti's taking to Paris."

"Ah! we're so proud of you, Ashmed, because you're going to Paris with the Monsieur."

"Ashmed is going to Paris because he does whatever Monsieur d'Argenti wants. Ashmed's going to Paris because he's very kind."

"And you'll go to school Ashmed, don't forget."

"Ashmed go to school, always with knives. Ashmed strong, must fight other boys. Ashmed always the strongest."

"Don't forget to thank the Monsieur, eh Ashmed? Don't forget. You'll get an education, you'll be rich some day, do you understand?"

"Yes, some day Ashmed wants to be cook, in Paris. Ashmed like Monsieur d'Argenti very very much, but Monsieur d'Argenti always angry at him, say he drinks too much punch."

"Have another glass, Ashmed, drink to your benefactor's health. We'd all like to be going to Paris with you. Do you think Monsieur d'Argenti will take us too, some day?"

"You too big. Monsieur d'Argenti like Ashmed because Ashmed small, very small, and nice, very nice. Give Ashmed another glass, Ali; Ashmed thirsty."

It was a hopeless ordeal for Monsieur d'Argenti to see Ashmed sitting at the bar on his high stool, legs dangling, for his feet didn't reach the ground. "Luckily he'll be too young for those sorts of places in Paris," Monsieur d'Argenti told himself as he saw the cherished child, the chosen one of his desires thus shared by everyone in all his mocking beauty, in turn laughing or pouting, shameless and without the slightest trace of timidity, but concentrated on his splendour, the velvety warmth that roses have and decked out in that magnificence that belongs only to those whom one has lost because they are, above all, not the property of others as they might seem, but the slaves of their own changing whims. Ashmed, laughing and drinking with his friends, had forgotten Monsieur d'Argenti. Antoine, overwhelmed by this indifference, did not know whether to smile at the child or rouse him with a slap, saying: "You bad boy, have you stopped thinking about me altogether?" No, that would have been too tender. Would it not be better to come to Ashmed, not too hastily, and suggest, touching his shoulder: "Would you like to sit with me Ashmed? You've drunk a little too much punch tonight."

"No," Ashmed replied, taking Monsieur d'Argenti's hand from his shoulder, "Ashmed doesn't want. Ashmed having fun with his friends. And Ashmed likes punch – it's good."

"Now, now, darling, come . . . "

"No. No. Ashmed doesn't want."

While he was striving to carry on an uncomplicated, friendly conversation with Ashmed, who had become more and more wilful and stubborn, Madame d'Argenti, running her hand through Mathieu Lelièvre's hair, was discussing Hindu thought with a young American diplomat named Peter, who was promising to come to see her in Paris. "Ah! how charming it will be to speak of all these things with you again, my friend," said Madame d'Argenti; "who else can I discuss them with?" Monsieur d'Argenti couldn't take his eyes off the small group composed of his wife, Mathieu and Peter, nor Ashmed who was drinking punch and abandoning himself to torrents of his lovely laughter before a group of admiring boys; Antoine felt that never before had he been so tightly entwined in so many tortures, all in a single night, suffering from love and jealousy, from turmoil and desertion — as well as from having given in too quickly to a creature who was born to conquer all the sensual pleasures on this earth, but scarcely intended for the lasting affection of a single master.

"It's late now Ashmed, perhaps you'd like to go to sleep?"

"Sleep? Oh no! You crazy. This is a party. Ashmed wants to see the party with the dancers from Morocco."

To show how important the celebration was, Ashmed took from his pocket a red sash which he tied around his waist and then, jumping off his stool, he began an indolent dance before Monsieur d'Argenti who, this time, could not control his irritation and said:

"We'll talk about it later, my friend. We'll have lots to talk about before we go to sleep tonight."

Antoine d'Argenti was, however, somewhat consoled when he accepted a glass of punch offered by Ali, the eldest of the boys, who told his companions that "Monsieur d'Argenti was doing a very good thing by taking Ashmed to Paris."

"Thank you, my friend," said Monsieur d'Argenti, warmly touched and courteous, "but it's quite natural and you know, Ali, I'll be sending Ashmed to one of the best schools in Paris, just as I did my own sons."

"You have sons?"

"And you'll see Ali, I don't doubt for a moment, they can't help but love Ashmed; he's an irresistible child and my sons will be delighted to meet him."

Ashmed, seeing that Monsieur d'Argenti had already forgiven him, clapped his hands and said: "Ashmed's going to Paris, Ashmed's going to Paris!"

"Basically, he's a fine boy," said Antoine d'Argenti to Ali. "Have you known each other very long?"

"Ashmed is my nephew," Ali replied. "We're all very glad

he'll be going to school instead of hanging around in the streets. Ashmed's too fond of fighting."

"I'll take away all his knives," said Monsieur d'Argenti.

"You're a good man," said Ali. "You take care of my nephew, you're a good father for him."

Suddenly convinced that he did indeed possess all these qualities even if until now few people had recognized them, Antoine took on a pensive air and modestly agreed, saying to Ali: "But is there anything one wouldn't do for one of these youngsters?"

When Antoine came back to sit with Madame d'Argenti, Mathieu Lelièvre saw a man who had been transformed, so lost in self-indulgence he seemed to have forgotten that Ashmed – and a few minutes later, Ali – had disappeared from the bar. It was because Monsieur d'Argenti, like the other vacationers already pacing the platform, was preparing for the arrival of the dancers, and the evening show always plunged him into an intoxicating enchantment. He asked himself some questions too: Where would he arrange for Ashmed to live in Paris? What would his children say about him? Would they like him? "The apartment is crowded, very crowded. He would need a bed, but perhaps we could put it in the junk closet while we're waiting – though it's rather damp in winter . . . But if he's with me at night I'll be too exhausted to go to the Bank, in the morning . . . The youngster will need some discipline too . . . yes, a rather strict education . . . " Surprised by the evening wind, Antoine allowed his wife to cover his shoulders with her woollen scarf.

"My poor kitten," she said, "you'll catch cold. And look at your face, the circles under your eyes . . . My poor friend, do you think you're still twenty years old?"

"Yes, tonight I am," he said softly.

"Here are the dancers. How handsome they are, what sensuality quivers in their barely covered bodies . . . Ah! Now we're living the Thousand and One Nights," said Madame d'Argenti, smiling, to Peter who had come and sat – but prudently – very close to her, letting Mathieu Lelièvre decide by himself to move away.

Mathieu thought with relief that the proof he no longer loved Madame d'Argenti was that he felt nothing when Peter appeared beside her, but out of instinctive competition he tried nonetheless to see what it could be about Peter that Madame d'Argenti liked. Perhaps Peter's superiority lay in his total lack of imagination? As he spoke little, Madame d'Argenti could say everything in his place, and he knew how to listen with that silent distress of disinterested people whose neutrality is absolute in all things, his wide statue's eyelids scarcely moving beneath the carefully tended helmet of his hair. Mathieu thought it must be reassuring for Madame d'Argenti to have her long monologues on religion end with the ritual dozen oysters and the bottle of champagne that Peter gracefully offered her, with the dream that she would soon clasp to her fiery breast a creature so phlegmatic who, happily, had a reputation for leaving generous tips everywhere. "I have a brilliant intuition about people," Madame d'Argenti said of herself and Mathieu thought that, once again, she wasn't mistaken. For Monsieur d'Argenti who had, momentarily, forgotten Ashmed's escapades – since he thought "what you don't see causes you less pain" – other memories, less caustic, lulled him as down below, on the stage open to the starry sky, the frenzied dancers paraded. "Why must we commit so many acts of madness for a single face? Of course that's the selective nature of passion!" But this oasis of reason where love was resting and even in decline would not last: Monsieur d'Argenti saw Ashmed come towards him, hopping and galloping and pouting serenely like a sinner without contrition. He was radiant and beaming and in his presence all other faces, even the handsomest dancer's, disappeared. Monsieur d'Argenti, his heart pounding, was captivated, but he lacked the strength to push Ashmed away when he came, subdued and ready to seduce again, and sat in his usual place – on Monsieur d'Argenti's knee. Meanwhile, a male singer dressed as a girl, with a bawdy voice that seemed to come from the depth of the cave of all the senses joined together for a single song, a single cry of the body triumphing over the mind, made merry on the stage; the voice seemed luminous because of the power of his animal felicity – so many supplications for ardour, such feline swaying – that Monsieur d'Argenti turned pale when he saw the soloist, his head shaven, tear off his turban and advance to greet the crowd; he wiped away a tear as though afraid of seeing his entire life stop then and there, at the sight of a vision that was so moving and so frail. This feeling that all life is precarious seemed not to touch Madame d'Argenti who, that evening, as she felt with relief – for her arms had been burned too harshly by the sun that day – the warm night wind along her scantily clad body, preferred to abandon herself to the present, thinking of the future only in order to enhance it with all the hopes with which she suddenly imagined her fate to be overwhelmed because in Peter she had encountered America, and America would come to visit her some day in Paris. But how long must she wait? When would the robust Peter, in Paris on a diplomatic mission and already, for Madame d'Argenti, a symbol of magical virility composed of gifts, sensuality, and money – "and why not," she thought, "it's all the same for a woman" – when would he cross her doorstep and then the threshold of her bedroom under the eaves? While she waited, Mathieu was still there, "but the chivalrous, ridiculous young writer" as she called him privately, sometimes – did he still love her? For Madame d'Argenti did not know how to explain the aggressive little flame in Mathieu Lelièvre's eye . . . Was he renouncing her already, and for so little? Why were others suddenly changing? "Ah!" she thought, "it's always like this, there's always someone who wants to thwart my happiness . . . " But soon she would have to go away, leave Peter and return to Paris and even see again the children she had forgotten and would have preferred "Yes, when I really think of it, never to see again." But the flight home was so turbulent that she changed her mind abruptly. Sometimes only the fear of death can tear from us tender sighs for those we do not love: Madame d'Argenti, like her husband sitting on her left, had neglected to fasten her seatbelt "Because why, my friend, tell me why one must always do what everyone else does in this world?" The desert crossing seemed so easy, and she had just admired "the imperturbable calm of the blue sky over Tunis" when the airplane, shortly after leaving the ground, at the very moment Madame d'Argenti was about to drink her first apéritif of the day, her eyes closed to savour it, began to tremble frenetically, then to plunge into the depths of the air as though trying to find its way; this caused Madame d'Argenti to say, when the eternity of fear had passed, "*Mon Dieu*, these people are so primitive one should never allow them to fly an airplane." For Mathieu Lelièvre who, like the others, had risked his brief existence, whose complexion was the colour of green apples, and who was sitting bolt upright in his seat apart from the others (for he had decided that morning to sit with Madame d'Argenti less often), death would have been swift and lonely but, he told himself as he wiped on his jeans the sweat that still soaked his palms, he had had the privilege, one last time, of observing human nature. If the airplane had continued to fall, these hundred men and women would have been flung into the middle of the sky, in the thousand fragments of an instantaneous putrefaction, virtually silent despite their impotent cries and dragging with them their cargo of rugs and pearls; Mathieu Lelièvre would have taken with him, to the gulf of his personal infinity of which he still knew nothing, the gluttonous profile of Madame d'Argenti as she prepared to drink her Dubonnet, at the summit of confidence in life just when all she loved with passion was about to be snatched away from her, the garment of her flesh being consumed as quickly and attacked by a flame as treacherous as the transparent blouse with which she had clothed and revealed her breasts that very day. Mathieu Lelièvre saw all that in the light granted him between this moment and his death, saw amidst the ruins of a Pompeiian disaster frozen in the sky the figures of Monsieur d'Argenti and Ashmed burnt to ashes where they stood as they surged towards the future, Monsieur d'Argenti preparing to open forgiving arms to his angel of evil, for to his last breath Ashmed could be faithful only to himself and his carnal inspiration, just as his affection for trade had driven him, even if the flight to Paris was only a beginning to be pursued with the German architect (the grey-haired adversary Monsieur d'Argenti feared so much, for Ashmed granted to greying temples weaknesses favourable to his own temptations), this man whose caresses he had known in the night, an exchange of candies and mischief the vision of which plunged Monsieur d'Argenti into such a white heat that he wouldn't have felt – just as he did not know fear, so preoccupied was he with love – the other fire creeping towards his ulcerated heart.

"Ashmed will go to Germany to see you some day, when he's bigger, but you'll buy me a big sabre. Ashmed wants a sabre."

At least in the muffled crackling of the general explosion Monsieur d'Argenti would have had the consolation of not hearing Ashmed murmur into his accomplice's ear, but as the motor did not explode the tragedy was held in check once more, giving way to the drama of Monsieur d'Argenti's daily expiation, an expiation he believed he did not deserve. "But," he thought, "only love can make us martyrs in spite of ourselves." Monsieur d'Argenti heard the words being exchanged by Ashmed and his architect, but when he saw Ashmed playing with a ball as he strutted down the aisle on one foot and then the other, the plane became as dubious a place for Antoine d'Argenti as the streets of Tunis or the shadowy bars. He made only one motion, opening his arms to his lost sheep, fearing that if he were to close them at this instant he would enter more distant forests of perdition.

The d'Argentis' return to Paris was quite normal, however, and Mathieu Lelièvre, who had tasted the company of others until he was satiated, appreciated for the first time in months the silence of his garret. He felt nostalgic affection for an old pair of boots standing in a corner and he pressed to his heart the letters from his mother and even those from Pierre-Henri Lajeunesse whose pomposity usually irritated him; he wondered why he had spent so much time far from the friendship of his books and the satisfaction of a job well done – all, he thought, "because of a woman who's unable to appreciate me." But he immediately regretted this thought: was he not removing himself too quickly from Madame d'Argenti? Had she not reproached him the previous night for being "like the others" and for loving her "so little?"

"It's because you and I have more or less separated," he had explained.

"We can love each other even after a separation; who's to prevent it? Love me, my friend, you'll see, the experience can only enrich you . . . "

But once Madame d'Argenti was back in Paris she had other preoccupations: from a telegram addressed to her husband she learned that one of her sons, who had run away to Italy, had just landed in jail in Milan; while the other, Paul, was still prowling around the kitchen in his apron, sharing some fish with the cats. Madame d'Argenti observed bitterly that "that illiterate hasn't become any more brilliant during my absence."

"Just think, my dear Antoine: even though you pay for a private tutor, the wretched boy is a disgrace to you, just like your other son. Yes, his tutor wrote me that he's a hopeless case."

"Hopeless in mathematics," said Monsieur d'Argenti, more conciliatory, "but I'll try to find another career for him. Couldn't you call your friends the Cordeboix? They have friends in Milan – important people, you told me; think of that, we can't afford to have a son in prison, even in Italy."

Monsieur d'Argenti also confided to Etienne, the evening he returned home. "When I think that they've put the youngster in jail simply for stealing a car, it's really too unfair! As for Paul, I have friends in the Navy, perhaps they'll take him . . . "

"He could always scrub the deck of a ship," said Etienne.

Monsieur d'Argenti was abruptly aware of his solitude. The loving freedom he had known in Tunisia had made him forget he was a father, but now all his responsibilities were crowding around him: Christian in forced exile in Italy, Paul in the modest cage of his kitchen, Paul, whose failures in mathematics seemed written on his face, which with disappointment, grew longer towards the bottom, suggesting the shape of a shoe. Then there was the third burden presented at moments of crisis by Madame d'Argenti. "Yvonne has never been so nervous; you know her passionate nature, my dear Etienne. Ah! it's too much for me, too much—what would I do without Ashmed?" Antoine d'Argenti was already wondering, though, whether Ashmed might not crowd the apartment. Ashmed and Madame d'Argenti together took up too much space to be under one roof. "What will Yvonne say," Antoine wondered, "when she sees that Ashmed has already carved a tree in the bedside table with his knife?" Antoine had envisaged this scene with terror so many times that when he saw Madame d'Argenti come towards him, her face crimson, when he heard the familiar voice pronounce this verdict: "That boy will leave or I shall . . . one of us must go . . . if he refuses to, no, don't exasperate me, Antoine d'Argenti . . . if he refuses, very well! I'll kill him, that's all!" when he heard these words Monsieur d'Argenti was astonished at his own calm as he said simply:

"I understand, my dear. You're upset, our children are causing us some difficult times."

"Your children aren't mine. I've always told you they'd bring you nothing but trouble. But don't look so worried: the Cordeboix will take care of everything."

"Even if it's proven that Christian is guilty?"

"What does that matter? You know very well stealing is fashionable nowadays . . . "

"And where will Ashmed sleep?"

"Why not in the rats' nest where you keep your papers? He used to sleep in the street, after all, and besides, think of it, who is this little guttersnipe you're imposing on us all? A thief, my friend, a delinquent . . . "

"Calm yourself, my dear, think of all the bills I must pay, be reasonable. My office is overflowing with them . . . and please don't yell, I have a dreadful headache."

Antoine d'Argenti hid his thinker's head in his long hands, asking himself through what iniquity he should be feeling so dejected after days of exaltation and serenity in the land of his desires. Even Ashmed, transplanted to Paris, no longer seemed the same. Weren't his cheeks rather broad? His eyes too wild, his hips heavy? "A school; I must find a school for him tomorrow morning, that will keep him busy." Madame d'Argenti's piercing, angry cries shook his temples again and Paul – the better to accompany the storm – was at the piano, where his discordant soul was languishing.

"Just what are you doing there!" Monsieur d'Argenti exclaimed, his hand sweeping the accumulation of bills off the desk and covering the rug with a layer of dust. "Couldn't you come and help me?"

"I'm composing, Antoine," said Paul gently. "I wanted so much for you to hear my latest composition."

"Another time!" Antoine cut in. "In any case, all your compositions sound alike."

"But I was thinking of you when I wrote this one."

"That's nice, child, very nice; but couldn't you prepare your little brother's bed?"

"What little brother?"

"Why, Ashmed! Haven't you noticed how tenderly he looks at you? He'd like to sleep in your bedroom."

"But I don't have a bedroom," said Paul. "I sleep on the red sofa, near the kitchen."

Monsieur d'Argenti was too harassed that evening to notice the hostility that already reigned between his two sons. Paul, the natural son – at least he had been naturally conceived by a mother who prided herself on being "unnatural"

93

– had no intention of sharing the narrow space in which he led his meagre existence "with someone of another race," as he saw it, moving his already expressive jaw in all directions, while Ashmed, whose filiation with Monsieur d'Argenti was more voluptuous in nature, had not renounced the always clean and perfumed father for "the son who never washed and whose feet stink like a corpse's" as he declared to Monsieur d'Argenti. "No, Ashmed doesn't like people who stink; in his country Ashmed goes swimming every day, Ashmed likes to be washed and brushed and the tourists like to wash Ashmed. Ashmed always smells good, never sleep with Paul because he smells too strong."

"Now, now, Ashmed," said Monsieur d'Argenti, "aren't you overdoing it a little? Paul washes too. By the way, son, did you wash yourself even once while I was away?"

"I always wash my hands before I serve dinner," said Paul with a dignified and wounded air. "You know very well that I have excellent manners, but Bonita refuses to wash my underwear. Ah! as Yvonne says, it's not the way it used to be; we have a different sort of servant nowadays . . . "

"See here," said Antoine d'Argenti, irritated, "I don't understand you, Paul. You've always been fond of your other little brothers, even when you were a child. They were often your playmates and even your bedmates when I didn't have enough space for them in my room. Why don't you like Ashmed?"

Paul didn't reply, but his young and already exhausted gaze took in the framed photograph of one of these "little brothers" on the piano; Ashmed, who always heard everything, even things people might have preferred not to admit to themselves, stood rigid, like an animal preparing to leap; it seemed as though he was hearing Paul announce in the silence: "The others had blue eyes and blonde hair; this is the first time you've brought home one of that colour." He was about to throw himself at Paul's throat, a knife in his hand, but Monsieur d'Argenti separated the two adversaries, holding the feeble Paul with one hand and with the other,

Ashmed, admiring despite himself the boy's impulsiveness: for if the one sometimes made him feel that he had pro-created death, with the other it was, rather, life that he experienced, the spasm of a secret resurrection. "But who could understand that?" he wondered, while Ashmed, more peaceful now, came and sat on his knee and Paul, grumbling, returned to his pots and pans. "Yes, who can understand the mystery of our choices and our tastes?" Antoine d'Argenti was sorry he didn't have the freedom to admit frankly to his colleagues at the Bank or to his family whose aristocratic grumbling made him fear for Ashmed, what he would say during an ordinary conversation with Mathieu or Etienne: that he had "a certain affection, a great deal even, for a young boy's ass." No, even if he were to announce it elegantly he could never do it, he thought, in a city where, without being talked about, nonetheless everything was done. He noticed for the first time, when Ashmed's woolly head was snuggled against his shoulder, that the child's skin, which in Tunis had seemed "reasonably dark," had, in the Parisian dusk, "a more chocolaty tint." Not that Monsieur d'Argenti's love for Ashmed was diminished because of this, he thought, but he suddenly had a foreboding of a whole series of mortifications he had not felt before and of which Ashmed, in his innocence, seemed even less aware.

Monsieur d'Argenti was accustomed to study the reactions of French society through those of his wife. If she exclaimed, upon seeing Ashmed in her boudoir ("She who is the personification of refinement"), Antoine thought: *Mon Dieu,* how dark the child's skin is!", if she herself, who was joined to Antoine "by the bonds of marriage, which still count for something in Paris," forgot that social grace – tact – and withdrew into disdain, what would be the reaction of others whom he did not know? Antoine d'Argenti remembered uncomfortably "some offensive comments" by a retinue of Frenchmen booing as they laughed in the salon of the hotel, shortly before they left Tunisia (for those whom they called "les boys" were at the time carrying their heavy suitcases to the waiting bus) "that dance almost without veils, lewd, you must admit, by a poor black prostitute from Tangiers." It was a very inelegant vision, thought Monsieur d'Argenti. Ah! Why did so many memories accompany Ashmed's animal nature everywhere, even when he was resting as he was now, dozing against Monsieur d'Argenti's shoulder and drifting slowly into sleep? Antoine heard the voice of his wife, encouraging her compatriots to remark:

"Watch her dancing; how disgusting! When those people are low they're truly low, If she were just black – but she's a whore besides, it's despicable! Come, Antoine, I can't bear this, let's go have lunch, there's time before we leave and it's included in the price of the hotel."

"We have our own too, at home," Monsieur d'Argenti had replied, to curb his wife he thought, but mostly to divert from his own weakness Ashmed's gaze, which settled on him in a fleeting flash of condemnation. Was Ashmed not saying at this moment: "You're just like them, you're the silent accomplice of all this hatred against my race."

"Ashmed thinks you people bad, very bad. Ashmed not want to go to France with you."

"Come, darling, I've already written my sons to tell them you'll soon be at our house. You can't imagine how thrilled they'll be to meet you."

"Is that true? They love Ashmed very much?"

"You'll see, in Paris."

Madame d'Argenti had started to make amends for her bad behaviour by saying to her husband, after devouring her enormous breakfast: "Wipe his tears and take this money to buy him some candies from me. You know very well what happens when he starts one of his crying fits. The little boy is quite an actor."

"People are cruel about things they don't understand," Monsieur d'Argenti thought, holding Ashmed's limp body in his arms, for the child's legs were dangling in the air.

"*Mon Dieu*, it's torn already. I've just bought him these woollen trousers. What shall I do with him? With Berthe writing to say that she needs new clothes for her lycée, and Christian in Italy . . . " However, as he had told Etienne that evening with conviction, Antoine d'Argenti was certain it was "better to love Ashmed than to be alone." Etienne always smiled when someone spoke of a kind of solitude that was not familiar to him; he had known the pleasure of nights with Monsieur d'Argenti but he had also fled from warm, grey mornings with the other man who, with the day, became "Yvonne's husband." And too, Etienne preferred not to think of the solitude that Antoine talked about. Mathieu Lelièvre had spent a long time living close to Madame d'Argenti's husband, just as he had lived close to the man's wife. Yvonne often went to bed with a song on her lips, but she rarely got up without some kind of fuss; and even if Antoine, like Mathieu, had in the course of the night experienced all the fires of Eros, Yvonne would appear in the morning with her coffee pot, her pale pink dressing gown open to reveal an energetic knee, furious because she had to start living again so early "among all these men who can't even heat up a bowl of coffee by themselves." Then the fires of the night would immediately go out, each one would take his place around the kitchen table, in the silence that follows painful decisions. Mathieu Lelièvre who, at the beginning of his affair with Madame d'Argenti, used to walk home, wondered what laziness caused him to be sitting next to her husband at this frightful hour when those who are dissimilar should not be seen by one another, offering to butter his bread when Monsieur d'Argenti replied, sulking: "No, I'm too late. I told Paul to wake me at seven, but as usual that boy thinks only of himself."

It is true that the d'Argenti family had gradually persuaded Mathieu to join them. "Yes, it would be so pleasant to eat together, *en famille*. Do join us; why not be comfortable?" but Mathieu Lelièvre so disliked Madame d'Argenti in the morning that he would have preferred to deprive himself of her presence. It was hard for him to get up, as he had slept for only a few hours, and when Victor the cat leaped from the window to his neck (the better then to melt into Madame d'Argenti's arms, meowing) it roused him too abruptly from his sleep. No, in the morning Mathieu, like Antoine, was not fond of life.

"Paul put out the wrong suit for me," Antoine d'Argenti told his wife; "it's winter, will you tell me why he's picked a summer suit? Does the boy even have the intelligence to tell the difference between the seasons?"

"I've always told you, you need a valet to follow in your wake. But I can't do it, Antoine, you're too demanding. Someone must brush you off and hand you your hat in the morning. Who do you think I am?"

"Don't shout, for heaven's sake don't shout!"

"I'm shouting because you're growing deaf, my friend, and that causes me a great deal of pain. Some jam for your bread? Paul, pass the jam to your father and you, Mathieu, make yourself useful, bring me the brush for his hat. *Mon Dieu*, what a life! I'll tell Bonita to put away your summer suits and take out the winter ones. Is it my fault if Bonita does nothing properly, even if that's what we pay her for?"

"We haven't paid her in two months, Yvonne, I must remind you," said Paul.

"Two months? That's nothing. She can wait a while longer. Oh! Antoine, my sweet, I was angry but I won't be any more. Could we have tea at five o'clock today, on the Champs-Elysées? I'd like to buy a few things with your . . . "

"You know very well that I go to Fauchon with my sister on Fridays and then we have tea together."

"Which sister? The Marquise? But I'm your wife; am I not more important than a sister?"

"You know very well that Fridays are sacred for us. We've been having tea together for twenty years. It's a custom."

When Monsieur d'Argenti introduced Ashmed to his sister Odile, thinking the Marquise would be so distracted by the exquisite care she lavished on her purchases at Fauchon's that she might not take the trouble to lift her veil and judge with her own beautiful shining – but severe – eyes, the quality and merits of the person to whom she was being introduced, that she might say, in keeping with her traditional reticence, as well as out of respect for her brother whose timid glance she would avoid as she contemplated a jar of peanut butter she intended to buy for one of her sons: "My friend, are you sure this merchandise really comes from America? It's the only kind François likes." Then, seeing that her brother was holding her shopping basket and not answering, she lifted her veil slightly, adding the expected phrase: "Another little boy you've magnanimously adopted, my dear Antoine? But you seem to forget you're not as young as you once were . . . Such responsibilities, my friend; I understand these things; I'm a mother, after all."

"I wanted to talk to you about your godson; not here, though, we can be heard . . . "

For as he followed his sister down the aisles of the store, Monsieur d'Argenti respectfully greeted someone whose face he recognized from a dinner party in his circle, and unlike his sister Odile he reproached himself for not being able at a given moment to place a name, a particle, on a nose or mouth which nevertheless showed every sign of nobility. "Come, my dear Antoine, that was Madame de Xavier, didn't you recognize her? You don't go out enough, my dear, though it's true she's aged a great deal since the death of Monsieur le Comte . . . "

"I'm sorry to hear of the death of Monsieur le Comte," Antoine replied negligently, placing his hand on a grapefruit his sister was offering him, "from Florida?" she went on, "and are these oranges from Morocco still fresh?" she asked as well. "Yes, yes," Antoine murmured, drawing Ashmed back to his side with his left hand, for the child's pockets were already bulging with stolen candies.

"That's bad, very bad," said Monsieur d'Argenti. "Look at those ladies and gentlemen in their fur coats. They have little boys too, but they never steal. Come now, put back that box of candy. There, what a good little boy, isn't he, Odile?"

The Marquise was concerned about the quality of some olives. "I want them pitted," she told her brother.

"And a few slices of salmon too?" Antoine asked. "Then we'll have tea. I simply must speak to you about our Christian; he's in Italy and unfortunately . . . "

"No, not here," she whispered.

"And you can have a mint syrup and a treat if you behave yourself," said Monsieur d'Argenti, trying to keep Ashmed near him with a grasp that was more firm than tender, for other delights were attracting the boy.

"Ashmed was in prison too when he was little, and the big people beat him. Look," he said, pointing to his scarred temple, "that's where they beat me. Ashmed's going to get even with them."

This confidence aroused Odile d'Argenti's interest, for as she turned to her brother she said with the sudden benevolence of an older sister: "My dear Antoine, you're really very brave . . . Or perhaps you're a saint . . . or else . . . no, I can't find the word."

Antoine took his sister's arm and they walked to their usual tea room, but he didn't take his eyes off Ashmed, who was frisking about in the cold rain. "Look," he said, "the child is so fond of life in the streets, of movement . . . The rain will soon turn to snow; Ashmed will enjoy that."

"There, I've found the word," said Odile d'Argenti; "yes, you're a born pedagogue, Antoine! Ah, this nasty rain; I'll call and ask my chauffeur to come for us." Then, warmly approaching her brother: "I'm really so happy to see you. It hasn't changed. Do you remember your first recital, when you were only twelve? *Mon Dieu*, what a splendid child you were!"

"So were you," said Antoine rather sadly.

"Why have you given up music?"

"Yvonne, don't you remember . . . " Monsieur d'Argenti began with embarrassment. "Yvonne has never liked the sound of the piano."

"My friend, I've always told you, you made a most unfortunate marriage. I don't want want to speak ill of that woman but . . . all the same . . . "

"My dear Odile, I beg you, don't exaggerate."

"But really, why did you marry her? Forgive me, but when I think of you, whom I adore, of my darling nephews and my niece in exile, so far away . . . "

"Come, my dear, you must get warm . . . "

Odile d'Argenti could not hold back a happy smile as, punctually every Friday, she walked, holding her brother's arm, into the tea room that bore the name, so sweet to her, "La Durée." It seemed to her then, as her brother removed her coat, that this place, because they came back to it together so often, was an extension of herself. Antoine, always moved to see her so beautiful, attributed his sister's well-preserved magnificence to the radiant health that no attraction, no vice, had ever touched. "She won't grow old, whereas I'll turn grey all by myself," he thought, lowering his eyes.

"Christian is travelling in Italy, you said?" she asked.

"No . . . not exactly . . . I must tell you the truth: he's in prison. No, don't be alarmed."

"The poor child!"

"The Cordeboix are helping a great deal; they have friends in Italy, but still I'm rather concerned. Could you try from your side? You must have some friends and . . . "

"I've always told you, it was a very bad marriage," Odile d'Argenti interrupted (then she ordered politely "two sandwiches and two teas"). "Christian, my nephew, in a . . . *Mon Dieu*, it's scandalous. His mother gave him to a nurse too soon."

"But she had to, she didn't like to hear him cry."

"Tell me, Antoine, is that normal for a mother?"

"No. But . . . Yvonne isn't like other women, she's an artist first of all, don't forget . . . "

"It's immoral!" said Odile d'Argenti. "A woman, especially a mother, must be able to choose: She may live only for herself, perhaps, but she mustn't sacrifice others."

101

Ashmed, meanwhile, was swinging on his chair, impatient to devour what Monsieur d'Argenti had called "a treat." He had already drunk his mint syrup and after making a few faces to amuse himself, he said to Antoine and his sister: "Ashmed was in prison too when he was little, just like your son."

"*Mon Dieu*, the child has a loud voice," said Odile d'Argenti.

"Softer, darling; his voice is changing, you see."

"Ashmed had lice and he only ate once a day. But one day a Monsieur from Europe came to get him. He paid for Ashmed. No more prison."

Odile d'Argenti, still thinking of her godson, wiped a tear beneath her veil.

"Don't cry; you're so sensitive."

"A nurse, when he was only two weeks old! Did the child ever experience a mother's goodness?"

"No, but he's been in the best schools in France," said Monsieur d'Argenti. "And thanks to our friends' influence I was even able to spare him military service."

"That's still not enough! What have they dared accuse the poor child of in Italy?"

"If I understood correctly, the police found him asleep one morning in an Italian car that didn't belong to him. They concluded that it had been stolen . . . "

"How unjust!" Odile d'Argenti sighed.

Ashmed turned over and over the thin sandwhich that had just been put on his plate. So that, he thought, disappointed, was a "treat."

"Come now, eat," said Monsieur d'Argenti. "You're always saying you're hungry."

"Ashmed thinks this is paper."

The Marquise looked at Ashmed with her beautiful eyes, seeming to notice suddenly that Ashmed was different from "Antoine's other boys" because of his "African origin" as she would say later, discreetly, to her brother, adding gracefully: "Your choices are more and more handsome."

But when Ashmed's charms were commended in his presence, Monsieur d'Argenti resembled those poets avid for praise who, when their work is glorified, still blush with humility; he murmured, his head in his hands: "How those we love wrench tears and sweat from us!"

"My poor friend!"

Then he began again, more cheerfully: "I'd like to show him the beauty, the greatness of France, visit our uncles' château with him. He'll find our architecture very moving."

"Do you think so?" asked Odile d'Argenti. "Who nowadays can truly appreciate the greatness of France? The war has turned us into creatures as fragile as any others; soon the nobility of their ancestors will be foreign even to our sons."

Antoine d'Argenti was thinking about Ashmed's education and when his sister placed her wasted hand on his wrist – thinking he was as close to her as he had been in the past – he thought she had never known him so little. Odile d'Argenti smiled at her brother, hoping he would share her regrets over a France that had disappeared forever; she looked back to a past opulence beautified by memory, but Antoine, forgetting Ashmed for a moment, reflected that "it would be more prudent to sell our uncles' château; we've all gone into debt to maintain that glacial château that's never warm, winter or summer, it's a luxury isn't it? We visit it only once a year, for Odile's children, in the summer. Yes, I'll speak to her about it next Friday, such indulgence after all . . . "

But Antoine d'Argenti could sense that he would never have the strength to impose such a sacrifice on his sister.

"You know we have a château in the Dordogne. We'll go to visit it together," he said to Ashmed, who wasn't listening; "we have a farm . . . "

"And ponds, like the prince in Morocco? Ashmed saw the prince in the newspapers."

Ashmed had not eaten enough; he thought of the pot-au-feu he would serve himself in Paul's kitchen. They never gave him enough big pieces of pork or lamb, he thought. "Because Paul no like Ashmed. Ashmed has his knife, for the meat. Paul gives the cats the best pieces. That's bad for Ashmed."

But their visit to the château was not as fruitful for Ashmed as Monsieur d'Argenti had hoped. "It's true that the poor child has no notion of our History," Antoine thought as Ashmed stared delightedly at a medieval sword, "which has likely cut off lots of heads," instead of at the family coats of arms; and he was saddened by the warlike penchant of the child in whose arms, nonetheless, Antoine had discovered more indolent preferences. Ashmed enjoyed stories of the Crusades, clapping his hands when he was told that "there had been many victims." Monsieur d'Argenti became concerned at Ashmed's bloodthirsty ardour as they toured the neglected estate together. "We need a gardener to look after the roses, and the chimney, yes, I'll speak to Odile about it, we must repair the chimney and the little tree I planted when Berthe was born has died." Long and solitary before the château lay "the children's snack table"; so many generations had moved about this table – the hundred-year-old trees still bore witness to them, covering the grass, rare in this season of frost, with their uninhabited shadows. Here, in the summer, through a period that had long seemed to Monsieur d'Argenti cut off from the tragic events of the world, an entire population of servants and attendants had come, at the slightest flurry, the slightest whim of the several people who had been chosen – for their race or their fortune – to experience each day the feast of this consolation. As Antoine d'Argenti looked over his estate, so deserted today (he could hear the sound of his footsteps on the path in the park, while Ashmed whistled by his side), he thought that he was alone now, like the eighteenth-century château, resplendent in its own light for only a few hours every year, when young lives came to rub themselves against its dry old stones. During those brief summers Antoine saw again, behind the faces of his nephews and grand-nephews, his own faces – those from the past, those that soon, like himself, would be but shadows of a world that had fled: even Odile d'Argenti was not the same young girl she had once been; although she now had all the authority of a grandmother she was no longer the one who called at snack time, telling him to climb down from a tree or not to run beside the pond, but rather, like a woman playing an-other's role in the theatre, she came out in her white muslin dress to give an order to an aged servant who had always been with the family forever, to bring to her a child who had accidentally fallen into the pond, to ask what time dinner would be served – for even if the time of the châtelaines was past, she proved by her supreme patience and respect for customs that the d'Argenti family was resistant to time, even though time betrayed them all.

Mathieu Lelièvre too had been introduced to the châteaux of France, by Madame d'Argenti, but he had insulted his mistress's pride and knowledge by betraying at every step how much more he knew than she did. "When I think that the poet Ronsard slept here, in this bed," he would sigh. "Yes, I know, Voltaire once admired this painting . . . " "Your head's filled with useless historical foliage," said Madame d'Argenti with annoyance. "What good is it? It's not even your history, it's ours!" for she would have been embarrassed if asked to name all the kings of France as Mathieu did during his peregrination through the past. "I don't like the past, so why should I like history?" asked Madame d'Argenti. If she did enjoy seeing Versailles again, it was mainly because she found it pleasant, reassuring even, to see herself wandering through the gardens, admir-ing her own dazzling reflection in the faded mirrors. In these places, marked with undying dust and boredom, she was tri-umphant as she saw so many things die while she was still there, adjusting with her small hand the hair her coiffeur had gracefully arranged that morning. And because she was accompanied by a young man with an ardent expression, "even if he's really rather foolish," the appearance of her person in this mirror seemed to her doubly flattering and rich in promise. And so Mathieu Lelièvre noticed, during one of these pauses at the edge of History, that Madame d'Argenti, suddenly transformed by her delightful mood, was smiling at herself, "an almost exalted smile."

"And may I ask why you are looking at me like that? Do you have any right?" Madame d'Argenti exclaimed quickly, replacing her calm mask of contentment with a bitter pout that was perhaps her true face. "Yes, tell me."

"Because it's rare to see you so satisfied."

When they went together to "Antoine's château," Madame d'Argenti, suddenly filled with doubts about herself and fearing she was not loved as she deserved to be, would assume the gentleness and modesty of the Madonna to please her husband. One could scarcely hear her live, she who usually roared so loud: a few minutes later, she would tell Mathieu Lelièvre that her sons were "only savages, who don't wash," but sitting beside her husband on the d'Argentis' terrace, she would murmur now, lowering her eyes, that "Christian and Paul were preparing to enter the Polytechnic this fall," that they were "kind, so kind, those youngsters," and that Berthe was "the most charming of modern young ladies; since she's been living in London there's even something English about her that's absolutely delicious and exotic."

At the sight of Madame d'Argenti successfully and harmoniously embracing all the feminine excellence the family expected of her, even raising herself to the role of mother, she who was so ill at ease in that role, pressing chaste knees together beneath her flowered skirt – she who liked to sit indecently everywhere – Mathieu thought that this woman who accused herself in her books of being "an unnatural mother" was perhaps less so in real life. Is it not more arduous, he thought, to reject one's children than to overwhelm them with love? Or else, on those autumn afternoons, those too long Sundays when sighing, she would accompany her husband to provincial châteaux, was it not Madame d'Argenti the writer who said to herself that she had "rejected forever the ties of a family and society," while the bourgeois woman resumed her place with the others? Perhaps, Mathieu thought again, Madame d'Argenti was, after all, merely a respectable woman, ordinary like all human beings, but capable of exceptional cruelty. One might believe, too, that when Madame d'Argenti told her sister-in-law that her son Paul was "kind, very kind," some part of her believed in this attribute, while the other reviled her for having inconsiderately held this same son up to ridicule a few hours earlier. Paul himself was touched when his mother softened her reprimand ("Ah! what a cretin, what a dolt! You ask him to buy a newspaper and not only does he come back without the paper, he doesn't have his bicycle or his keys either.") with this tender crumb: "Yes, but you're so kind, I must admit that." It was as though this one word had the power to wipe out for him, for a long time, all the hostile phrases that every day pierced his flesh.

Ever since Mathieu had started loving Madame d'Argenti less, he was more sensitive to the subtle differences between her truth and lies, but at the same time he was aware that he resembled more and more the heroes of her books: he too, like the characters she had created, was sliding from one ambiguous appearance to another, bereft of any ethical feelings. And like the author's conscience, was he not giving in to a strange apathy? Often too – for Mathieu Lelièvre was living not just Madame d'Argenti's book but his own as well – he was more struck by the physical than the moral woman. But nothing is less capable of lying than the body, and when Madame d'Argenti plunged into her hip-bath, which she alone in the household had the courage to occupy, her pink and happily self-sufficient nudity lapped by the water and a great deal of soap, Mathieu, whom Yvonne had invited to "read to her a little" perched on the toilet seat, could not doubt that this woman, who seemed sometimes always to lie to him everywhere else, in this place told only the truth. For never had she been so carnally visible, even when he selected some uplifting passage for her, and Madame d'Argenti, with a naturalness that for Mathieu was greater than Nature's, slowly caressed herself, saying defiantly: "No one can do that for me as well as I do myself," directing into the labyrinth of her sex the spray of a shower that was flexible for that very purpose. Mathieu was not resentful that she should love herself so much, but how could she forget that he was there? And was she also forgetting the other person she would become at five o'clock, on the d'Argentis' shady terrace, the other woman who, as she chatted with Odile d'Argenti, would give in to a *frisson* of bigotry? Mathieu told himself that a woman like Madame d'Argenti, who said of Ashmed that "he has the dirty habits of his country; just imagine – I caught him urinating on the quay the other day," little knowing how uncivilized her own habits were. For she had begun in Tunis (unlike Ashmed in Paris) to pee as she stood in her tub, suddenly transforming herself into a boxer with legs apart, while Ashmed stood gracefully beside the Seine, following with a velvety eye the silver arc of his deliverance. But although Monsieur d'Argenti had been able to persuade Ashmed that "one doesn't do that in Paris, out of respect for the Seine, you see," Mathieu Lelièvre drew from Madame d'Argenti only a shameless smile and her condemnation of "an excess of modesty that's useless in Paris." Did Madame d'Argenti, in these spontaneous attitudes, still resemble the worldly woman confiding to Peter, in Tunisia, "the sensual pleasure of religious ecstasy?"

Mathieu Lelièvre was spending more time alone in his room reflecting, and it seemed to him that his heart was cooling, his mind becoming more lucid. He walked around his bed, thinking he must "never see that woman again," but if she came to fetch him "to go for a walk in the Bois de Boulogne with some friends, come now, you can work tomorrow . . . " he would obediently give her his arm, not because he loved

Madame d'Argenti but because the feeble rays of the winter sun would warm his limbs, chilled to the bone, better than the heater in his room, he thought. In Madame d'Argenti's company one did not walk, one ran, and this invigorating sport sometimes ended with a hot toddy by a roaring fire, in a café that had, like so many other places, witnessed the beginning of their affair and would perhaps witness its end as well. There, Mathieu Lelièvre would have at least the satisfying sensation – thanks to the rum and the aroma of warm milk and the effect of the flames that sharpened Madame d'Argenti's face in the shadow – that although the affair was dying he, Mathieu Lelièvre, was still alive. But today, when they stopped for a toddy after their walk in the Bois de Boulogne, Madame d'Argenti touched Mathieu's ankle under the table with the tip of her boot, throwing herself into what she called, frankly, "an inconsequential flirtation." Turning her inconstant head from side to side she smiled, showing her small teeth in all their whiteness ("so much cupidity for such a small mouth," Mathieu thought now, reproaching himself for his lack of pity, for was Madame d'Argenti guilty by being less lovable to someone else when to herself she was as lovable as ever?), the row of perfect teeth expressed, however – or so Mathieu thought – all that the rest of her person never wearied of showing, for she was so comfortable by the fire that with only her foot and the edges of her trembling lips, she gently allowed her fresh-blown sensual needs to drift away to the neighbouring tables and the young people sitting at them. One of the boys, stirred by her intrepid yet indolent behaviour, rose to his feet; his broad arms burst out of the two holes in his sheepskin vest, and he came to drink greedily from Madame d'Argenti's glass, telling her ironically: "To your health, Madame!" Mathieu Lelièvre thought suddenly: "She's only using me for one of her writer's experiments!" This notion was strangely intolerable, but he forgot that Madame d'Argenti was afraid of being persecuted in the same way by him. Had he not realized that since their return to Paris, Yvonne d'Argenti no longer allowed him to go up and wait for her, alone, in the evening, in her room under the eaves? She had told her husband of her suspicions: "Where is my green note-book? That girl has robbed me again . . . "

"What girl?"

"Berthe, she's always . . . "

"But my friend, our daughter is in London!"

"Then he's the only one, Mathieu, I mean. Ah! now I understand why he enjoys coming to see me so much . . . He wants to make off with my notes, that's it! I felt a presence, Antoine; I was at Madame Colombe's and we were talking about her will again; and rest assured, she's changing nothing, she's as stingy as ever, she's just been offered millions for her latest erotic story. Well! Can you imagine, the film rights don't interest her, she wants twice as much . . . In a way it's probably better like this, my friend . . . If some day, but that would be quite unlikely, wouldn't it? . . . In any event, if one day she were to remember me in her will, but we mustn't dream . . . In any event, I came home then and I felt that a presence, that had no respect for me, had entered my room, yes, in the silence and the dark, yes, someone had disturbed my papers on the table . . . It can only be Mathieu, for the moment at any rate, who else comes into my room under the eaves?"

"Victor."

"Victor respects my papers, Victor would never dare to read what I write in secret."

"Perhaps he doesn't know how to read, but I find his muddy paw-prints all over my writing-paper. And you know very well that Victor's no ordinary cat," said Monsieur d'Argenti, "he's yours."

"Don't say anything bad about my darling."

"Couldn't you teach him some manners?"

"He's a very old cat; it's too late."

"Yes. Very, very old," Monsieur d'Argenti repeated, suddenly filled with sentimental sorrow. "Ah! that cat knows so much. Dear Victorine . . . "

"Please, I beg you . . . Victor. Don't bring him down to the level of my sex."

"Do you remember when she killed her own daughter with one swipe of her paw? She didn't like motherhood, poor cat. He suffered a great deal, he's so old now and so lonely . . . the children cried so much, poor things!"

"Why do you feel sorry for them? Aren't they perfectly all right today?"

"Poor children," said Monsieur d'Argenti to himself.

If Madame d'Argenti was performing "an experiment in degradation with a literary goal" on him, Mathieu Lelièvre thought, was it not time to leave her? Was he not master of his own life? No, he would no longer telephone her, and if she rang at his door he wouldn't open it. He would take a trip (yes, like Antoine d'Argenti, he too was receiving troublesome bills), he would write his book, he would forget "that woman." But it would be a pity never to see Ashmed and Antoine d'Argenti again, or pursue with them a story he had finished with Madame d'Argenti, for they too were characters in another novel, another drama of which he did not yet know know the dénouement. Antoine treated Mathieu with distant cordiality, sometimes even asking his advice, particularly since Ashmed's education in Paris had taken a disturbing turn.

"My dear Mathieu, couldn't you, who are so good with children, come and take care of Ashmed this evening while I'm at the Bank, at my meeting? You understand – I can't take him everywhere. The other night at the concert he slashed the upholstery of his chair with a razor and yesterday it was my wife's leopard cape . . . I know he's rather old to have someone stay with him, but you could amuse him by taking him to a café and buying him ice cream."

Monsieur d'Argenti could go out "with his mind at rest, for Ashmed will behave himself," but as soon as Ashmed started running through the streets of Paris, Mathieu began to regret accepting Antoine's suggestion.

"We're going back to the café so Ashmed can play in the shooting galleries. Will you lend me a franc?"

"Already? What did you do with the francs Monsieur d'Argenti gave you at the house?"

"Ashmed spent them after school. For cigarettes."

"You know very well Monsieur d'Argenti doesn't want you to smoke when he isn't there."

"Ashmed isn't obedient, it's true. Ashmed obedient some days yes, some days no. Today, no. Like Paris – one day rain, next day sun. Ashmed's like that. Ashmed will win lots of money with the big people, on the machine in the café."

Ashmed led Mathieu with his dry little hand. Everywhere, in all the cafés on the rue de Buci, which he seemed to have known since his early youth even though he had been in Paris only a few days, he had "friends," "brothers"; he had met Ali in the souks, Mohammed in the mountains, and Antoine d'Argenti had observed, not without melancholy, that for Ashmed true brotherly paradise was always to be found away from the white race. Ashmed often told Mathieu: "Monsieur d'Argenti good father, and Ashmed good son," but if an argument darkened the honour of one of his people in a café, if in a bar on the boulevard Saint-Germain the reputation of one of his Arab brothers was slighted, he would renounce in a twinkling all the benefits he received from Monsieur d'Argenti, the better to partake of the integrity of battle; he would have slashed the neck of this white Father whom he knew, however, he could not live without, yield completely to his passion for justice, even though he never emerged from battle without a bloody lip for, as the smallest of the big boys he wanted to defend, he was often the first to be hurt.

"Have you been fighting again? What will Monsieur d'Argenti say tonight?"

"He'll make a compress for Ashmed. Ali punched Ashmed in the jaw. Ashmed not happy. Ali made a mistake, he wanted to fight the big Parisian who called him a nigger, but he made a mistake and hit Ashmed who was defending him. Give Ashmed your handkerchief, it's bleeding hard."

Ashmed's friends lived outside Paris, in shantytowns, and often they ate only once a day; when Ashmed left them in the evening to join Monsieur d'Argenti who was waiting for him at the door of the Bank, a shadow of regret would pass over his face. Perhaps, he thought, while Ali was taking him to the bathroom to wash his face ("Hey!" Ali told him, "don't let Monsieur d'Argenti see you with blood all over your face; you'd better stop fighting for me and making so much fuss; promise, Ashmed, otherwise you'll end up in jail."), perhaps Ashmed was thinking then that at this season of his life, if he had been at home with his own people, he would have been able to eat (and sometimes feed his mother and sisters too) the harvest of his thefts from the fine gardens in his city, where he could use his charm to exploit those who abjectly exploited his people, but those hours of freedom seemed so far away . . . Today, Ashmed was dressed superbly and Ali, who polished the shoes of passersby, still wore the rags of his past life.

"Ali, you never steal like you used to, from the tourists in the gardens?"

"No, Ali doesn't want to go to prison in France. Ali would be lonely and unhappy. Ali doesn't want that."

Then, even though he had scarcely had time to dry his tears, Ashmed let himself be carried away by the exuberance of his serene nature.

"When Ashmed was little, very little, he went to the gardens in Tunis every day to see the pepper plants in flower and he'd eat oranges with the tramps, and when a tourist came by, hop! Ashmed was there and he'd say to the Monsieur, do you want to come and read your paper and sit on the bench? And the Monsieur would be hot and while he was reading, Ashmed and Ali would do his pockets."

Ashmed fought at school as well. In the midst of his monetary discourses (which already caused him considerable concern, before he left for the office in the morning) Monsieur d'Argenti would receive telephone calls from the Director asking him to "come and get his son, the one who is

113

violent, very violent . . . " for Ashmed had discovered the imploring magic of this phrase when the Director called him in for a thrashing. "Call my father, at the Bank."

And nearly every day the Director called the Bank, while Monsieur d'Argenti seriously considered taking Ashmed out of school, but every night he told him, when he put him to bed in the "rats' nest" (the vestibule where Antoine, as his wife suggested, had placed Ashmed's cot among the scraps of paper): "Darling I want you to learn to read and write in our language; it can only be useful to you, so go back to school and promise me you won't fight any more."

"Ashmed promises on his honour. But stay with me and tell me a story."

"I can't, I have too much work. I'm three months behind in my correspondence. Close your eyes and sleep. I'm working just next door, I'm not far away."

But Ashmed's nights were so agitated by nightmares that Monsieur d'Argenti had to get up from his chair several times and go back and forth with a glass of water, a compress, aspirins. He was so distracted by his solicitude for a single being that he forgot everything else – Madame d'Argenti, who was waiting for him after the theatre, and the letter he was writing to Christian, still in Italy, behind bars. The unfinished letter sat on his untidy desk. "My dear little boy," Monsieur d'Argenti had written, "today's youth is a victim of all the disorders in our endangered society and you, my unfortunate son, are one of the innocent victims who has been cruelly punished . . . " But Ashmed's cries during a bad dream: "Yvonne is bad, she said 'Throw Ashmed out on the street,' Ashmed's scared, very scared . . . " these cries from the depths of a soul in distress that Monsieur d'Argenti saw in Ashmed only at night – for all day long Ashmed laughed – snatched Antoine d'Argenti from his torpor and he ran immediately to Ashmed and took him in his arms, telling him: "Come now, you're a big boy, you know it was only a dream. You know Yvonne loves you as much as I do."

"Ashmed thinks she's a witch. Ashmed's afraid. The other day she pinched Ashmed's arm, when you weren't there. She very bad. She wants to take you away from Ashmed."

"Go to sleep now, I'm here."

Antoine d'Argenti, who for so long had doubted that his wife could be guilty of anything at all, "for judging those we love is a little like judging ourselves," he thought, told himself as he reassured Ashmed with tender gestures – the glass of water he gave him to drink, the pillow he replaced beneath his head, the ceremony that follows fear of which Ashmed no longer wanted to be deprived – that in the past he had heard the voices of Berthe, Christian or Paul exclaiming in the same defenceless tone: "Yvonne pinched my arm when you weren't here, Yvonne . . . Yvonne . . . " and that perhaps this time too she was guilty of what they accused her of doing in their dreams. Antoine admitted that "in the lobby of the hotel in Tunis that morning, it's true that Yvonne seemed to share some prejudices with the other French people, yes, a certain racism. But wasn't the black woman dancing before us a little provocative?" Since Ashmed had been living in his house, though, Antoine had had ample proof that what had been latent in Yvonne in Tunisia had become, once she was home, the expression of a visceral animosity she didn't even conceal from those closest to her. Monsieur d'Argenti thought sadly: "She doesn't like Ashmed because he's himself," but he knew that even if Ashmed had been French, white, "but from a lower social situation," she would not have liked him any more. Mathieu Lelièvre had protested, in words this time, in the hotel lobby, against Madame d'Argenti's "spirit of segregation," judging that henceforth this woman "would be unworthy of his love." But was he, like Monsieur d'Argenti, not protesting first of all for himself, protesting not the humiliation of an entire people but in order to raise himself up? For it was disappointing to have for a friend a woman who was elegant only on the outside, who was not even discreet enough to veil her vulgarities a little. He thought too, though, that the hostility and animal contempt Madame d'Argenti was so proud of were covertly transmitted each day through human actions, in a hidden manner. He too was a sort of Madame d'Argenti, he told himself, but more secretive; he was waiting for his own crimes to be revealed, for in the illusion of what is good we know ourselves so little. It was in evil, he was learning, that reality is to be found. He had written to Pierre-Henri Lajeunesse that henceforth he would fight against "all forms of racism." It is more convenient, however, to express such a principle than to put it into practice. He was already inclined to protest and he realized that he did not even have the patience necessary to defend such a simple charitable axiom; and he who flattered himself that he liked moderation now quarrelled everywhere he went. And if he defended the right of a Senegalese student to exist, in a train from Paris to Chartres, if he gave up his place in the restaurant car to a visiting professor at Lyon, an Indian, he would arouse everywhere clucks of indignation and furious wounds; he had been tolerated when he was silent, but he wasn't liked when his demands were uttered aloud. Antoine d'Argenti himself, victim of a social wrath that society itself preferred not to name, enjoyed a sexual bigotry of a superior order. Did he not speak emphatically – referring to his youth – of "the birth of a certain pederastic flower"?, of the dawn of his "Socratic career"? If a couple of men who were getting on in years were to confide in him, he would exclaim with disgust: "*Mon Dieu,* I know nothing of that," thereby marking the physical difference, the distance that could exist between his sphere, bathed in the sensuality of the springtime of boys, and the sentimental winter of two brave fifty-year-old men who, nonetheless, loved each other with the same acts. Everyone, if he can, congratulates himself on the fruits of his harvest, even when it is gathered in secret. Antoine d'Argenti, too, denounced any manner of loving that was not his. Moved to tears when Ashmed called to him in the streets of Tunis: "Monsieur the foreigner, do you want some flowers? No? Do you want tea at my brother's house? No? I know what you want then, you want little boys." Touched by the graceful child who placed this palm leaf at his feet, seizing like a prey all the truth that lay in his soul, the same man mocked the "vulgarity of transvestites, the coarseness of effeminate men who dress like women," and his contempt for these people who were, nonetheless, very like himself in the homogeneity of their appetites, could be boundless. But perhaps he fiercely tackled these fragile resemblances to himself to gain relief from some poisonous insult that had caught him by surprise one day . . . who knows, in the Métro, at a street corner, where he had nevertheless been seen clad in all his protective measures and accompanied by his wife and children. At that moment of hatred, everything had become disastrous for him when an unknown voice whispered in his ear: "Hello, you old queer . . . " Other insults passed through his life like invitations to please or to seduce. Antoine d'Argenti would never forget Etienne undressing in a hotel room in a small village in Egypt and saying to him in a surly voice: "So, d'Argenti, do you like my cock?" Even if Antoine d'Argenti was able to reply: "Aren't you a little too proud of your body, my friend?", hoping thereby to clip Etienne's feline claws, he recognized that there was a sort of offering in these words, "even if it's a little rough" for how could he have guessed that Etienne, who was always correct in his hunting garb, would become when he was abroad, when he was naked, so Gaulishly insolent? How many times, having a drink in the evening, during those hours when Mathieu Lelièvre, resting from his passion, delighted in Antoine's male presence in the d'Argentis' apartment, how many times had Antoine declared that "throughout history, pederasty has been the destiny of superior men"?

"And you, my dear Mathieu," he added gravely, "why do you like women? What do you find in them? Of course you love Yvonne, that's quite different . . . "

If Etienne was there he would leap into the conversation, saying: "Ugh! women are too soft. Like pillows. I like them hard and hairy . . . How dreadful! As for your wife, d'Argenti, I wouldn't sleep with her for all the tea in China; she's a bitch and really rather common."

"My friend, I beg you, don't you have any respect for me?"

"I've always told you, d'Argenti, I loathe her. She's your worst enemy."

"You forget that she was generous enough to pay for our trip to Egypt when you were fifteen."

"Ugh! common, I tell you."

"Be quiet, Etienne, I can't bear this, you're really hurting me," Antoine d'Argenti replied, sincerely saddened by "Etienne's innate coldness, but you must understand him, Mathieu, he's a child who grew old too soon."

Like Etienne, however, Antoine d'Argenti also called women – with the exception of his wife, from a moral loyalty that seemed to persist through every outrage – "common," and did not hide his contempt for them. But though he was to be heard everywhere sowing his curses on "the inferior and stupid sex," it was, Mathieu thought, only so he could hide and forget all the tortures inflicted on him by a woman singled out from all the others – Madame d'Argenti.

Etienne said frankly: "Have no illusions, Mathieu; Antoine d'Argenti and I spit on women."

And perhaps the truth lay there too, in these few words from the mouth of an angel, a few words that were nonetheless coated in venomous saliva, for Mathieu Lelièvre had finally learned that the instinct for discrimination was everywhere, that it was undying, and that contempt and hatred were for many men and women the only expression on this earth of their sinister way of loving.

Odile d'Argenti took leave of her brother and left the tea room, saying it was urgent "to go and buy some *foie de canard* for my husband before the shops close. You know, my dear Antoine, my husband can't exist without his *foie de canard*." Antoine d'Argenti understood this wish: he sometimes ran all over Paris so he could offer his wife the indispensable cheese "that she simply can't deprive herself of without pain," and Mathieu who had also been called on to satisfy pressing needs for a certain cheese, "a certain wine that Yvonne d'Argenti couldn't get along without," had worn out his shoes running the same sorts of errands. It seemed overwhelming to him (and how hypocritical of him!) shortly before Christmas to drop into the hand of a *clochard* dying alone in the street, a handful of francs and centimes, keeping the rest for alimentary satisfactions that did not seem part of the same moral realm: very often Yvonne d'Argenti would nibble at one bit of cheese, then at another, and then, disenchanted, send Mathieu or Paul "in search of savour, taste, because that's what I'm looking for, not the cheese itself. And that's what you can't understand, Mathieu, and why not? Because you underestimate me and you've always underestimated the refinements of our country," sending him to some distant crossroads where, indeed, the cheese truly did exist, soft and mouldy and asking only to be eaten by the stomach of a connoisseur like the d'Argentis. Odile d'Argenti was deeply fond of her nephew; she had sobbed when she learned that he was in prison but the *foie de canard* whose perfume she already smelled, the *foie de canard* that was the expression of a ritual, not greed, between herself and her husband, erased even the memory of her nephew and the presence of her brother.

"Don't forget your godson," said Antoine d'Argenti as he waved goodbye to her.

"How could I?" she replied, then promptly disappeared.

"Ashmed's hungry."

"Again?" Antoine asked, leaning towards Ashmed whom he had somewhat neglected.

"You always talk with your sister and Ashmed hungry. Ashmed always hungry."

Christian arrived noisily one morning, head high but looking haggard; he tossed his knapsack, which seemed as grimy as he, against his father's piano and as Antoine d'Argenti offered a paternal embrace he could only utter, looking at him: "Don't touch my piano, son, you're so dirty . . . And how skinny you are! *Mon Dieu*, where have you come from?"

"Your disgusting friends, yes disgusting, the Cordeboix, do you really think they got me out with all their connections? Well they didn't."

"Now now, don't talk that way about our connections. They'll be useful to you one day."

"Some peasant came to defend me and what a hell of a mess it was! They kicked me out and I've even got a police record now. That country's full of assholes!"

"My poor son!"

"And who's that?" Christian asked, pointing to Ashmed who was nervously shifting his weight in a corner, "another of your street urchins? I'm telling you right now, Antoine, he's not to sleep in my sleeping bag."

"Who'd want to, child? Even your sister Berthe doesn't and she's a woman . . . a young girl. She says it smells terrible."

"Him never wash either," said Ashmed, laughing.

"And tell that one to be quiet," said Christian. "I don't want to hear him."

"Now now, why are you in such a bad mood?"

"A month-long stretch is enough to put anyone in a bad mood, isn't it? All I had to eat was ravioli, every day, and they made me wash the walls and clean out the shit house. Really, Antoine, it was disgusting; would we do that to a worker in France?"

"Ashmed liked prison," said Ashmed, "except for the lice in his mattress and the flies that bit his nose when it was too hot."

"Now Christian, be nice to the child," said Antoine, introducing Ashmed to Christian. "He's one of my sons and I respect him just like you."

"You and your sons!" said Christian. "I have no desire to be nice. Why didn't you leave him where you found him?

France is rotten and dirty, and Aunt Odile is just as rotten ..."

"Christian, if you please!"

"Disgusting. They're all a pain in the ass – and their money didn't even get me out!"

"You think only of yourselves, my sons. Yes, you're all alike. But I insist on some respect for the family. You're back now, so let's celebrate."

"Like the prodigal son, eh? Is there anything to eat in this place? I'm famished."

Christian was already prowling about the kitchen, sniffing Paul's absence with displeasure. "And where's the other one? I want him to cook me a steak."

"Your brother hurt his foot in a bicycle accident; he has to go to the hospital every morning for his bandage."

"The idiot! Always something cracked. If it isn't his head it's his foot . . . So now he's got a bandage and he'll be moaning and groaning and dragging his foot for weeks. Disgusting."

At this moment Yvonne d'Argenti and Mathieu Lelièvre, who had argued all night, appeared in the vestibule. Madame d'Argenti was still bleary-eyed from the quarrel and her face looked so threatening that Christian who "didn't speak reasonably" as his father had just remarked, but "bellowed," was suddenly silent, open-mouthed, his grey eyes, ringed with shadows ("Ah! Madame d'Argenti's eyes," thought Mathieu Lelièvre), lighting on his mother's face with affliction.

"So it's you," she said, noticing that Christian was home, standing there before her. "I thought you'd disappeared forever."

"Yes, it's me," he said complacently.

"They proved your innocence, I hope."

"No, because I was guilty. Look, it can happen, but those bastards – even though it was a first offence, right away it's a police record."

"How shameful," said Yvonne d'Argenti, irascible again.

"Did you ever think of your father? A delinquent, that's what you are, and *le tout Paris* won't waste any time before they realize that we have a degenerate in the family."

But Christian suddenly remembered that he was angry too, even though his father, already late for the office, was mutely pleading with him to add nothing more. His pleading, and the silence that followed it, were between Antoine d'Argenti and each of his children in their mother's presence, and everyone was surprised this time to hear Christian reply: "Two degenerates," he said loudly, "you and me. And you too, Yvonne, you have a police record. Do you think I don't know?"

"Be quiet," said Yvonne d'Argenti, turning red to the tips of her delicate, already pink ears, "not in front of a stranger, not in front of him . . . "

"I don't give a shit about your love affairs," said Christian, glancing quickly and indifferently at Mathieu. "In any event, they're always changing."

"I forbid you to accuse your mother in my presence," said Antoine d'Argenti. "You're making her cry, look . . . "

"Those tears are just an act," said Christian.

Mathieu Lelièvre felt some remorse: perhaps it was because he had never seen Madame d'Argenti curled up like a little cat, smothering her sobs in the sofa cushions. He was accustomed to tears, but not to these spasmodic sobs, and so he approached her with humility and placed his hand on her shoulder. But when she felt his touch, Madame d'Argenti bellowed savagely: "No, don't you touch me! You don't love me any more, at least that's what you told me all night long. Go, then! Leave me alone. Oh, Antoine, I'm so unhappy."

"You know very well that I love you," said Mathieu.

"No, no one loves me!" Yvonne exclaimed, clasping her hands, "except for you, my dear Antoine." Then she turned to Christian, with fat tears still trickling down her cheeks. "You, you thief, you traitor, what do you have to complain about where I'm concerned? It's your sister who told you about my police record, wasn't it?"

122

"No, my grandmother. Everyone knows you mistreated your children."

"Well, let me tell you one thing, you retarded moron. I'm the one who accuses myself, quite shamelessly, in all my books, just as I do in the salons of all our friends. I tell them, 'I can't love those whelps.' With your father's intelligence and my beauty I expected to produce geniuses, not imbeciles!"

Madame d'Argenti had the gift of astonishing her audience, Mathieu thought. In her lethal monologues to her sons she might resemble Agrippina, but a few moments later she was betraying her heroine for another in an outburst that could only be described as "maternal"; she sprang to her feet and flung her arms around Christian's neck, kissing him fervently. "Is it true, my dear one, is it really true?" she asked in a pleading voice. "Did you really suffer so much because of me?"

"It depends on the day," Christian replied. "When you weren't infatuated with someone, everything was fine. We ate three meals a day. But when you lost your head over whoever was laying you, we were the ones who paid for it. We'd hang around the Seine, wandering about like beggars. That was how the Social Assistance people found us that day . . . "

"But I'd taught you to make salads and omelettes," said Yvonne, distraught. "It's all because of those immigrant maids who left us one after another."

"Let's talk about omelettes," said Christian. "Do you think a four-year-old child can make an omelette? That's how we ended up in the hospital, covered with burns . . . "

"Poor dears, my poor little children," said Yvonne d'Argenti. Then, looking at her son from the perspective of time passed, she said, after a moment's reflection: "No, I have no pity for you. You're tall and well built today. Look at yourself: do you look like a martyr?"

Christian was about to pursue his recriminations but they heard scratching at the door and Paul's choked voice saying: "Shit, my foot hurts."

It was early morning and nocturnal disorder still reigned in the d'Argenti apartment. Antoine had slept little, not just because of Ashmed who was "so affectionate at night, but also because the sound of the barges on the Seine drives me crazy." The comical sight of Paul pushing before him his foot decked out in a bandage the size of a cabbage, even though it was a vision of unhappiness and perhaps the only sign that still existed of the d'Argentis' past unhappiness, made everyone laugh, beginning with Madame d'Argenti who exclaimed: "Now our illiterate son's a cripple!"

"That's not funny," said Paul sullenly.

"No, it's very funny," said Ashmed, "you always comical with your sore paw."

Paul dragged himself into the kitchen, grumbling, and closed the door. At the window that opened on the court-yard, Victor was standing with his front paws on the sill, watching the snow fall. When he saw Paul he moved his head, expecting to be cuddled, then meowed happily. "You want your breakfast too, do you?" asked Paul. "But it's different for you," he added gently. "You're probably the only friend I have in the house."

Mathieu Lelièvre now spent entire weeks without seeing the d'Argentis, but Madame d'Argenti's reproaches haunted his solitude. "You're terribly ungrateful and your behaviour's quite reprehensible, after all we've done for you. But don't be so sure of yourself, my friend. Thanks to my friendship with Madame Colombe I can put an end to your career if I want . . . Who are you in the world of French Literature? Simply a foreigner, an adolescent. I know a good many critics who want nothing more than to kill off youngsters like you." But did these written reprimands (for Madame d'Argenti had taken to writing to Mathieu Lelièvre when she discovered that his door was closed to her) not come because Mathieu had brought them on himself by telling his mistress: "It's finished, we must break it off?" At the beginning of their affair he had thought that the flaws in the woman he loved so much were separate from his own; today he thought that he possessed all human vices, and that Madame d'Argenti, in the image of her own life, perhaps had the insidious mission of approaching people in order to snatch away their innocence and thereby reveal them to themselves: and so, he told himself, it was not she whom he loved less or more, it was what he had learned about the degradation of his own character that he disliked. "I can destroy your life," said Madame d'Argenti, but Mathieu didn't listen to her. "Who can kill the things of the spirit?" he kept asking himself, for reassurance. "No, one can mutilate bodies, humiliate and wound them, but not the spirit!" But perhaps it was too soon to judge the prophetic ravages of his work that Madame d'Argenti talked about. Indeed, he was still the "observer" of a certain generous France that was as yet unknown to him, but his affair with Madame d'Argenti had made him, like so many others, in their loving submission, "a case of possession, a case of sickness." And the only observation left to him was to discover just how sick he was.

Mathieu Lelièvre thought he would never see Madame d'Argenti again (had she not advised him through a missive that Peter would soon be in Paris?), but she came to him one evening, entered his room without knocking and began to read some manuscript pages scattered over his table, saying as she stared at him with a steady smile he didn't know how to interpret: "So our little friend is back at work, is he? Another novel? Yours or mine? Be careful, life repeats itself . . . Well, it's not so bad. A certain talent, as I've already told you. Do you want to come out with me? For the last time, yes, if you'd enjoy it . . . The De Marchais have invited us for drinks, with Antoine and the child. I'll tell you some entertaining things about the De Marchais — for a writer must understand everything, even what is ugly. Come now, it will be the last time. You don't need me any longer and I don't need you. But take advantage of it, because without me the door to 'our world' will be closed to you now. You'll still have your cafés, of course, and the little provincial Frenchmen you're so fond of. Are you coming?"

125

Curious about this "last evening in 'her world'" Mathieu agreed, but when he saw Madame d'Argenti on his arm, wearing her fur cape, he was certain (and perhaps it was a deliverance) that this woman had always been foreign to him: how could he have imagined her "small and defence-less," she who, in her high-heeled boots, now seemed "large and commanding?" "Yes," she said, still smiling with singular persistence, as the taxi took them to the De Marchais house, "these friends – not yet friends, perhaps, but they will be in time, that's what Antoine and I hope, because they have a magnificent château at Tours. Ah, yes! I was going to tell you about them. He was a collaborator during the War; poor De Marchais was nearly killed under the eyes of his son who was only four at the time. What a scandal, don't you think? Just because of some pamphlet against the Jews. Don't we have the right to hate whom we please? But I'm forgetting you hadn't even been born yet . . . Ah! what a life we lead in Paris, and what a marvellous city Paris is at night. So the poor man, Julien, had to leave by the roof to save his life, all before the eyes of his son, poor child. Yes, as I was telling you . . . "

Mathieu Lelièvre now looked at Madame d'Argenti with horror: was he dreaming or was she really speaking quite calmly, frivolously, about "the war . . . our friend De Marchais, the collaborator?"

"How can you associate with people like that?" he asked, indignant, but Yvonne d'Argenti answered his indignation with a smile.

"Yes, you were lucky enough to be born late, outside of History in a way."

"But they're criminals."

"What are you saying? Antoine and I associate with all sorts of people, and the past is far away." Then she added, suddenly furious: "What right do you have to shame and remorse? You haven't seen Europe awash in its own blood. You don't even have the right to think about such things. Criminals! You're exaggerating. Who isn't a criminal in these difficult times? Believe me, you'll see, they're absolutely charming, and their consciences are clear . . . And the little one who witnessed all these atrocities – is he the son of Julien's wife or his mistress? We don't know – we let these things pass. He has a military career cut out for him."

For the last time Mathieu Lelièvre entered the spacious interior gardens; their paths, as well as the long corridors in the De Marchais house, were lined with statues. All was luxurious, gilded, covered in velvet as at the d'Argentis, but the velvet here was a slightly faded grey that embraced in its circle of warmth men and women who, although they were dressed like people one encounters in the street today, represented, despite themselves, the past. Mathieu wondered, as he saw them clustered in their peaceful society life, whether each one truly represented some dishonest action, some vile act performed in the past, in a time the naked eye of the present could no longer see. Or were these distinguished individuals concealing their barbarism behind a veil, which risked opening at any moment to reveal their crimes? Julien was an old, still handsome man, his son an officer with piercing eyes, while his wife looked like a big painted doll, with her blood-red lips. She glanced about her, tolerant and tired, for her husband's mistress, sitting opposite her, still possessed what she had lost: a taste for life, and the insolence and vigour of those who feel that they are loved, whose sensual powers are still able to attract adulation, even that of their enemies. And so in this family only Madame De Marchais, Julien's wife, still wore a mask of funereal passion (and that, Mathieu thought, was perhaps because she was suffering in the present more than the others) that belonged to another period: this woman had not passed through time as flexibly as those close to her, and the face that Mathieu saw before him could well be not the face of tragedy but of a sort of death that habits were unable to bury.

Everyone was drinking cocktails, talking about the flu

127

that was raging in Paris, at times evoking "the good old days, during the War . . . "

"Yes, don't you see, it was a good time," said Yvonne d'Argenti, "because we were never sick."

"Indeed," Madame De Marchais replied, "we never ate our fill, so we had no trouble with our livers and we avoided the discomfort of appendicitis. Our only danger, death, was with us everywhere. We were afraid of nothing."

Mathieu Lelièvre listened to them, thinking that all his life he had had the illusion he had been "born good" and that he was perhaps no better (only different) from the d'Argentis and the De Marchais. But why did he shudder when Madame d'Argenti told her friends that she didn't like "Jews, Blacks, you know what I mean, Antoine, I can't help it . . . " Did he shudder from a feeling of shame for her, or because he sensed that in this world one always participated in other peoples' spinelessness, even if one used extreme means to combat it? Yvonne d'Argenti, who felt pity for no one, could say of Julien: "Poor man, luckily the Resistance didn't bring him down," and Mathieu Lelièvre must recognize that "evil people too, alas! are entitled to pity," a pity that was perhaps the reason for many murders. But suddenly he felt certain that if he was trembling with horror in the presence of these people, he might very well become, like others, "their Jew," "their Black." He wanted to take with him, far from these people, Ashmed who was wandering guilelessly among the statues, trying to make two huge bassett hounds, panting and suffocating under their burdens of portliness, jump up and join his game.

"Now, now Ashmed," said Antoine d'Argenti, "don't bother those poor beasts, they're old."

"Ashmed thinks they're pigs. They eat too much."

"Ashmed has the misfortune to be too outspoken," Antoine d'Argenti said to Madame De Marchais, indulgently.

"But the child is right," said Julien's wife. "Venus and Apollo are heavy: it's old age and comfort, and laziness too, what can one do? And they're always eating. I've even hired a young Spaniard to feed them and take them for their walk every day. For we must deprive them of nothing when the end is so near."

Julien interrupted his wife to ask Antoine d'Argenti: "Why do you exhaust yourself for that child, my friend? Couldn't he wait on tables in a restaurant or wash dishes?"

"No, I want to spare him that," Antoine replied. "I'm fond of the child, I want to try another school . . . He's so intelligent, perhaps too much so. Now come and sit with me, Ashmed," he said severely (perhaps he, like Mathieu Lelièvre, understood that in this house Ashmed's existence was threatened . . .). No, you mustn't touch the flowers, they're fragile, they live in a greenhouse."

"What's that?" Ashmed asked, his round eyes staring at a horde of small glass objects on an old table.

"Be careful," said Madame De Marchais, "be careful dear, those are tiny sculptures, miniatures. We've had that collection for years. They're so frail and they come from so far away, you can't understand, you're too small. But you see, we love these objects, these miniatures, these things; we respect them because, like little children, they sleep very lightly."

Ashmed didn't understand his hostess's monologue, but he came and sat, as was his custom, on Antoine d'Argenti's knee.

"Ashmed won't wash dishes. Ashmed's going to be a cook in Paris," he said in Antoine's ear.

Antoine d'Argenti did not reply. A glimmer of sorrow came into his eyes.

"At times, my dear," he said to Madame De Marchais, "I feel like your bassetts – tired, very tired. But like them I drag the weight of my life with me everywhere."

II

The rain and winds of the Parisian winter were accompanied by a hail of bad reviews that fell on Mathieu Lelièvre. His book had been politely castigated when it first appeared: now he was being ruthlessly massacred. Mathieu admired his detractors' style and erudition ("Who is this Québecois false Candide, this Proustian soul on a visit to Paris . . . ?") and as he wrote to his mother "with his elbow on the café bar," henceforth he would travel "to the pleasant France of our ancestors, for every day I strike up friendships with café owners from every part of France and I know that provincial France — so dear to your heart, *chère maman* . . . " And so he dreamed, pen in hand, stomach hollow (for if he wrote to Pierre-Henri to borrow a little money it would be an admission of the failure of his love life in Paris), ceasing his writing only to "taste another local wine with one of the regular customers, an old Norman woman, a concierge by trade, who could be your sister, *chère maman,* and although it isn't yet noon she has introduced me to the 'stirrup cup.' "

"There was something about you in the paper this morning, Monsieur . . . "

"Lelièvre, Mathieu Lelièvre. I told you yesterday. Call me Mathieu."

"Yes, I know; I've noticed that Monsieur comes here every day. They didn't speak very highly of you, but then they rarely do in Paris. The picture though — it was very impressive! You looked very solemn on page three . . . And you can feel the intelligence, eh!"

But later while drinking "a glass of *vin ordinaire*" with Juliette, his Norman friend, who was still wearing her bathrobe under her coat, her feet in her husband's slippers ("I borrowed them from my old man to cross the street"), Mathieu heard a less favourable tribute.

"I think, young man, your mug looks better in the paper than real life. Yes, quite frankly, since we're among friends, I didn't see what was written underneath; especially because I don't know how to read, but that's nothing to get upset about, it's like the dead, they always look better in their coffins."

The weeks passed and Mathieu Lelièvre thought with relief that he would never see Yvonne d'Argenti again. But why should she still interrupt his pleasures, why was he pursuing her? She was no longer sleeping in his bed, however, as she had been yesterday, or examining – sometimes starting at dawn, if she were in a stormy mood – his every action with an expression laden with threats. What was this shadow of Yvonne that was taking so long to go away? If he suddenly turned around as he was walking down the street, was it not she who followed him, wrapped in her cape, was it not her offhand laugh that echoed in his ear? She repeated what she had told him during their farewell evening at the De Marchais: "You've decided to leave me? Why not? You'll remember me, Mathieu, I'll make you suffer. It's not essential for me, you know, to see you . . . "

And if his novel slowly disappeared from the bookstores, it was perhaps because she had also told him: "I'll cause you a great deal of harm."

Why was she afraid of breaking with him and why did he fear this woman who was nothing more than a "ghost filled with sinister things?", he who had lived beside her for months without fear? "I used to call her Madame d'Argenti and my attitude was often that of a slave. Today, she's only

Yvonne, Yvonne d'Argenti." From then on her Christian name rose up within him like the memory of a strident insult. "Yes, Yvonne who has always humiliated others – her husband, her daughter, her sons. She's drunk their humiliation and it intoxicates her." The Christian name that had crowned an angelic face (but who knows, he thought, perhaps the face was still sleeping in some far-off drawer of innocence) was today part of a head "born in the world of serpents" he observed coldly. And yet, Mathieu Lelièvre thought, had Madame d'Argenti, imperious and beautiful, who imposed on even her intimate friends the social distance of *vous* (this same Madame d'Argenti who had awakened in Mathieu an idolatrous passion), had she even felt the metamorphosis from "beloved" to "least loved" overcome her? Was she not what she had always been – Yvonne d'Argenti – without the slightest deviation from the fate that had carved her to be this way forever? Mathieu remembered a confidence Antoine d'Argenti had shared with him like "a bad omen" of what he would one day learn from his mistress. Antoine was chatting with Mathieu in his smoky room, as was their custom, when he suddenly confided, eyes sparkling with tears that this time he could not contain: "You know, I've lost so many things in this house. I had splendid photographs of all the children I've loved; if you'd seen them you would have understood how happy we were together, and the limpidity and tenderness of our associations that nothing can define, for they contain no desire for domination, but I've lost them . . . How, I don't know, I've never known . . . I'd hidden them in a safe place but one evening when I was looking for them so I could show them to a musician friend I couldn't find them. Someone had burned them perhaps, I didn't dare to think of it . . . No . . . But it's so disturbing . . . In any event, my friend, the most painful thing was that a long time ago I also lost someone I adored . . . Years before, the children were all small . . . I'd surrendered to a feeling of pity for an orphan child who seemed doomed to spend his life in a home for delinquents

. . . At ten, the child had already suffered so much, he'd been beaten and ridiculed. If you could have seen the desolation in his eyes . . . The police were looking for him too, and this didn't happen in Tunis but here in Paris. I adopted him. He was all alone in the world; but as soon as the child began to take some pleasure from life, to sing and enjoy himself like a child, to play with my sons, Yvonne became very hostile towards him. I could see in his eyes the same fear he felt for the police. What was happening when I was away, while I was at the office? I could never find out from him. He began again to be silent . . . and that expression of humiliation . . . Why? I know that my wife, out of jealousy . . . no, I dare not believe it . . . but jealousy is a curse, it can turn the finest person into the most cruel . . . I think of that child constantly, even in my dreams. I see him, yes. One day the child ran away . . . when I came home from work I didn't find him in his customary place, sleeping in my bed, huddled under the covers, waiting for me – because I never managed to send him to school. It's wonderful, a child waiting for you . . . No, one evening he wasn't there . . . not in the courtyard or . . . anywhere. They searched everywhere, in the Seine . . . everywhere, but he was never found."

If Mathieu Lelièvre was afraid of meeting Yvonne d'Argenti it was not only because since he had stopped seeing her she had assumed, in his eyes, the face of a sort of fatality which had led him to a cul de sac (first that of seduction, then that of selfishness before which he saw nothing but a series of victims); if she appeared to him in dreams, in the middle of the day, in store windows, might it not be, he wondered, because he was still afraid of yielding to her charm? Did she not enjoy a power of which even she was ignorant? Could he not compare himself to Antoine d'Argenti who, although generous and sensitive to justice, had agreed, by uniting himself forever to his wife, to trample inexorably on what he loved most in the world – children? Love had no more made Mathieu a hard man than it had made Antoine d'Argenti a patricide, but both, in their way, seemed to have come out of this strange alliance with their integrity profoundly weakened. These were questions Mathieu Lelièvre would go on asking himself for the rest of his life.

But when night fell in Paris and indolent youths came to the muted light of bistros to collect their thoughts, to read or argue in low voices, Mathieu – who, like Yvonne d'Argenti carried notebooks with him everywhere – suddenly began to write, and he discovered that this was his "true passion" and that "all the rest was merely an adventure in the world of desires, and therefore doomed in advance." The two people philosophizing fiercely at his side became "immortal" for him, in his lust to write – they and all he saw and heard. Ah! Why did the critics who complimented him only for the shadow of "a promising talent" not notice that even without talent one may be gifted with the eye and memory of a giant? Yvonne d'Argenti herself denounced Mathieu's "anomalous photographic memory, it's monstrous, I wouldn't want such an instrument! I still prefer to buy paper." Yvonne d'Argenti had to know of her heroes "not only their bank accounts, but all their sexual obsessions . . . " which were of little interest to Mathieu. He would have preferred to confuse genders and sexes, but he never forgot a face, the intonation of a voice. Thus he had only to write in his notebook, "At the Café des Hardins d'Assas, two old men . . . " and twenty years later, he thought, he would hear again the old men muttering away, quite close to him, their big hands crumpling their caps: "You've got the fog following you and everything's just dandy. Then one day it hitches itself to your wagon – and that's called death."

"I've always said, life's made up out of what you can't do, that's what life's made out of. Death's for tomorrow . . . but you should never get married. Why bother? It's what a man does to escape from time, don't you think?"

"Let me tell you . . . You get married because you want some property, and then there's your work. And one day the girl's gone, your future's dried up, and you don't love her any more but there's the children . . . No, we don't even know why we're alive!"

Yvonne d'Argenti had often told Mathieu that she had "no memory for human conversations, it's all such an infernal uproar in my head . . . " and it is true that she had quite often deeply distressed Mathieu because of this flaw, this almost spiritual lack that made her at times a torture victim, blocking her ears with her fingertips, haunted; it seemed that some distant sound made her this way, a breathless, enraged sound that pursued her.

The two old men went on chattering, tasting the delights of reason, and Mathieu Lelièvre, bent over his notebook, saw as though reflected in a mirror the smiling face, the first face that had welcomed him "in the small Parisian apartment filled with shadows" of the woman he wanted to see no more: Madame d'Argenti. She was there, and he was writing about her; she approached, she came towards him "on that warm autumn Sunday." He slammed his notebook shut, folded his arms and remembered the reviews. "No," he told himself, "not even an unusual memory can console you for not being a genius." But after he had closed "the d'Argenti album" what would remain of those who had been for him in this city that he loved, only "faces, voices" he had not yet learned to know? As his memory poured out before his eyes its urn of details and incoherences, he felt consoled by her again, for did this memory not perform all the labour he need only write down later? He saw once more the intimist, furtive scenes he had sometimes tasted until they were worn away: stopping at the Gare Montparnasse where, as he was tying some rope around his suitcase (which had just cracked beneath the weight of his books), a concerned mother speaking with an obese abbé waiting for his train, of her "dear son Rolland, yes, Monsieur l'Abbé, I'm very worried about him, I fear the temptations of Paris . . . Ah! Monsieur l'Abbé, what Providence has brought me to you?" Then, the abbé's plump hand patted the worthy woman's shoulder: "Come, come, more evil things are done in the country; oh yes, that's the way it is . . . " And who in this world besides Mathieu Lelièvre knew that the abbé and

"Rolland's mother" had been quickly brought together by a seemingly distracted eye and so entered the kingdom of the immortals? And what had become of Rolland in Paris? Could he be in this bistro, bluntly ordering a "café crème" from the owner, expecting of others and of life "every favour; for you see, Monsieur l'Abbé, he's my only son and I've pampered him too much." Or Rolland might resemble Lucien, a young Breton intellectual Mathieu had met on a train from Paris to Quimper; Lucien, who in his native village was movingly sincere but who, when Mathieu saw him in Paris a week later, had been disconcertingly impolite. Lucien had imitated, in word and gesture, everything Mathieu today deemed to be "so odious, just like Yvonne d'Argenti." "You must be like the Parisians or simply not exist at all," Lucien seemed to say to Paris, rejecting his cotton smock and patched trousers for a silky sweater and velvet jeans, speaking insolently to everyone, even when he stopped at a *tabagie* to buy matches. Lucien listened to no one, except perhaps his own muffled snoring; he had read everyone, "everything that's being read in Paris just now," seen all the films. He was vehement when a taxi driver accused his people of being "backward, slow; those Bretons are so muleheaded!" But he could not come to their defence except through assimilation to a French élite that he scorned with all his heart; he talked like them and covered his body – massive but beautiful – and his accent that might betray his peasant origins, with a flimsy patina beneath which were real treasures he allowed to die. In the train compartment, sitting across from a lawyer and his wife who were closely observing not Lucien, but Mathieu, whose boots were muddy – "like a crude country chap," they murmured – the two young people did not talk but, in accordance with the habits of Lucien, who urged his friends to yell louder than he, they howled. For a long time Mathieu Lelièvre still heard in his memory the grunting of "that Frenchman who knew everything," who began every sentence by sighing with disenchantment: "Yes, I know . . . I read it in *Le Monde*" or: "Ah! you're going to the Côte Sauvage . . . I've been there at least a hundred times . . . it isn't bad" while his lips moved to form a smile describing awkward boredom. At the Côte Sauvage Mathieu was ecstatic as he sat on his rock "before the fabulous beauty of the setting sun," while Lucien, stretching his heavy legs on the sand ("Damn! I got my suit dirty! this beach is filthy!"), dressed as he did in the city "to show my friends that they know about clothes in Paris," grumbled sluggishly: "Not bad . . . this scenery, though it's better in Spain. I was reading in *Le Monde* yesterday . . . " but Mathieu had stopped listening; the shrieking of the gulls, the sea both calm and agitated, even the presence of Lucien, "an authentic Breton" hidden beneath his city clothes, all were miracles of the moment that helped him understand how Proust, as a young man, one day quite different from this one, on a stormy evening, had nearly died, suffocated by the beauty of the power of the sea.

"So there's still nothing happening in Quebec?"

"Nothing?" Mathieu cried into the wind. "What are you saying?"

"I'm saying nothing, damn it! And it's the same every-where, the same shit everywhere! What's the use of going away? Travel? It's the same shit everywhere! You know we were in a train that was nearly derailed? Yes, something about a bomb. What are you looking at? The water? The birds?"

Lucien, seeing it was hopeless to try to lead "that Québécois peasant" into the cerebral competition where he had served his apprenticeship in Paris, stared with his blue eyes – liquid blue like the sea – at the corpses of two gulls lying at his feet. The beak of one was partly open and its claws were interlaced in a final movement, stiffened in its mortal agony.

"Filthy pollution," said Lucien. "They're even stealing our beaches! Do you know that Britanny is about to be invaded by military installations? No, you don't know, of course, you don't read *Le Monde*."

They walked back, through small isolated villages already shrouded in the evening fog. "I loathe that," said Lucien, "it's bad for the health. It's so damp! I'm already starting to cough." And he began to do so, draping about his powerful neck a red wool scarf bought in Paris, which he cared for in an almost maternal way. "That's quality, do you understand?" When an old prostitute going home on her bicycle passed them, she shot them a shameless smile that reeked of wine. Lucien spat in the grass and called Mathieu "an asshole of a foreigner" because he had responded to her invitation with 'Bonsoir, Madame!'

"That's not done in Paris," said Lucien.

"Let's go have a beer 'Chez les Celtes,' " Mathieu suggested, as he saw beneath the roof of a low house a happy group of drinkers from the farm. "I see a light over there."

"Yes, I know the place. It's not bad, but it's full of drunks. The only thing I can drink is fine cognac, not that loathsome beer."

Workers in overalls were standing at the bar drinking. A fisherman whose face bore the scars of his trade, the marks of frost and wind in the creases of his brown skin, drank voraciously, along with his still young wife who was dressed very soberly, two, three, four small glasses of *eau-de-vie*. Mathieu Lelièvre remarked to Lucien (even though Lucien wasn't listening) that this evening village meeting reminded him of Van Gogh's paintings "because of the thin yellow light from the ceiling, you see, and the earthy colour of the people's hands and faces." But as he spoke he noticed that the fisherman, who all this time had been holding a small package under his arm, was opening it and taking out some oranges. His gesture, as he held out in the twilight fruits that suddenly gleamed like gold, changed the whole scene for Mathieu, a scene he wanted to describe painstakingly. And what followed dazzled him even more: the fisherman, who had, perhaps, bought the oranges on his return from a fishing trip, or received them as a gift, had the loving inspiration of using them to stroke his wife's cheeks. Did this delicate gesture belong to the man with the ravaged features, "that lout," as Lucien called him, blowing puffs of Gitane smoke out of his fleshy mouth, or did it come from his erotic Celtic ancestors? The old salt with the leathery cheeks and tufts of white hair sticking out of his navy cap went on slowly stroking his wife's cheeks. "It's good, isn't it?" he asked in a gruff voice, and Mathieu noticed that the woman he had barely looked at when he entered the café was suddenly beaming. She became radiant under the effect of a light that was timid at first, but her cheeks were now the colour of Lucien's, a bright, burning pink.

But Lucien, who would soon forget Mathieu, never knew what a compliment he was paying his friend when he asked him in a burst of modest enthusiasm "if he might by chance like to have supper with a Breton family." Mathieu felt at that moment that he was "predestined" to meet Lucien's family, and the two of them arrived like brothers at nightfall, so damp from the fog, so obscure to each other – Lucien bringing with him a bundle of dirty laundry and Mathieu a few books – that when Lucien's mother switched on the electric light in the kitchen it cast a startlingly bright beam that fell like a stream of milk over the frosty grass and they looked at each other for a long time without recognition while Lucien stammered to his mother in the dark:
"This filthy fog . . . It's me, *maman*."
"I put out the lights because of your poor uncle. He's just skin and bones . . . if you only knew . . . Your uncle Jean-Marie, you remember? the one who's dying . . . They opened him up at the hospital but there was nothing they could do, the whole inside was rotten."
"Ah yes, that one," Lucien murmured, pretending he hadn't understood.
"We've been expecting you for months," said the mother. "Your sisters are here and your little brother, in the big room. We've made a fire. We always expect you on Friday night. There's hot soup and potatoes and . . . "

"It's all right, *maman*," said Lucien, "he's a pal of mine," he added gravely, pointing to Mathieu. "Yes, Canada . . . you know? America? Understand?"

"There's hot soup," said the mother. "Come!" Mathieu had noticed in the distance several scrawny trees and the walls of the farm. Now dogs came running towards them, barking. He went under a sort of stone portico that Lucien called "the pig sty. Watch out, everything's falling apart here." And suddenly they were in the big room, standing by the warmth of the fire, putting their boots near the embers that were heating potatoes and the rabbit stew from the night before. Lucien's sisters surrounded them and Lucien assumed the virile duty of introducing them to Mathieu.

"The biggest one, standing by the table, is sixteen. She's Julie, the oldest. And the other one, with pigtails, is Solange. The little redhead at the back is Suzanne. And the other one . . ."

The eight girls could scarcely move in the cramped space their mother still called "the big room." One of them, Marie, was washing her hair in cold water, her back to the group of sisters. Suddenly she turned around and you could see her blonde mane and the water streaming down her face.

"And Marie who never behaves like the others," Lucien went on. "She's washing her hair again to go to the ball tomorrow."

"And your little brother?" Mathieu asked.

"He has an earache," said Lucien's mother. She pulled down a blanket on the only bed in the house and an adolescent's curly head appeared. He exclaimed: "Did you bring any books, Lucien?"

"He has an earache," said Julie. "He's been a nuisance for four days now, we can't sleep in his bed."

"Yes," said Lucien, "a book by Mauriac: *La Pharisienne*. You asked me for it, remember?"

But the child didn't reply; he hid his head under the pillow.

"He has a fever," said Lucien's mother. "We should send for the doctor. The nurse comes once a week to give your uncle Jean-Marie his needle, so we can ask him to come here at the same time."

"He's a real nuisance with his ears," said Julie.

"Yes, but those are needles for death," said Solange.

"No, they're for pain," said their mother. "These boys are hungry; they must eat. Set the table, girls. The soup's still hot and if it isn't eaten it'll go to waste."

"Mémé says papa's going to bleed the pig soon. Is that true, maman?" asked the sick child.

"You go to sleep," said Julie.

"You can see he has a fever, he's a little delirious," said the mother.

"How's Mémé?" Lucien asked.

"No change, your grandmother's always the same. But Pépé drinks too much *eau-de-vie*. She had to keep him inside yesterday. He hollered all day long, then he went to sleep. When a man's drunk it's almost as if he was asleep, and when you're asleep you've got nothing to complain about."

During this conversation between Lucien and his mother, a gentle intimacy began to prevail in the room and Mathieu Lelièvre, touching the head of a young cat under the table, then that of a second, even younger, as he brushed against the damp muzzles of cats driven mad by the smell of soup, told himself, feeling infinitely grateful to life: "I'm at home here!" even though he knew that this expression – like so many others – like the stars that twinkled briefly in the sky over Britanny (at dawn, the fog and then the rain would send them away) would not endure. Gradually the eight sisters, even Marie with her hair starched stiff by the icy water, gathered around Lucien, rather like the dogs and cats around the soup, as they sniffed the odour of their brother who was so clean, so haughty, so stilted in all his wool; as they stood close to him they listened and listened, fingertips playing with the hems of their aprons, and they exchanged singular looks with one another that seemed to say: "That's him, the man."

"Will one of your acquaintances have room for the little one?" Lucien's mother asked as he was taking a bottle of "sparkling wine for important occasions" from the cupboard.

"What little one, maman?"

"You know, Julie."

"Ah, yes! there's always a place for a maid . . . in fact I have a friend in the 16th *arrondissement* . . . her parents are looking for a maid . . . not so bad . . . five hundred francs a month."

"No," said Julie, "I don't want that. Paris is too far away."

"You'll go," said Lucien's mother firmly. "What can I do with a girl in the house, especially when she doesn't like the farm or her parents' work?"

"I'll go, maman," said Solange. "I'm almost fourteen now. I'd like to be a maid for people in the sixteenth . . . "

"I can't feed them all," said the mother. "Your father gets so irritated at your sisters. Too many girls. Ever since your uncle Jean-Marie's been so sick, your father's only got his horse to talk to . . . I don't count, you know what he's like . . . women, he never speaks to them."

"How is the horse?" Lucien interrupted.

"Getting old, son. Like all of us. And his poor legs hurt, just like mine."

"But maman, you're still young."

"A horse can be exhausted before his time," said the mother. "I told you girls to serve the men. What are you waiting for? Why are you standing there staring at the rain?"

"It might turn to hail," said Julie.

"Then it will freeze and we'll lose our garden, we'll lose it again. Can you hear Pépé yelling outside?"

"That's the *eau-de-vie*, maman."

"Mémé will bring him in if he's had too much to drink."

"How are things at the Post Office?" Lucien's mother asked.

"Not bad. We're going to have a strike. The more mail gets lost, the happier I am. What rubbish, all those people writing letters . . . "

"It isn't your salary from the Post Office that pays for that fancy get-up, my boy. You certainly must know people in high society."

Lucien blushed and did not reply. As his sisters put the plates on the oilcloth-covered table and served him and Mathieu, Lucien grabbed one potato after another with his clumsy hand, devouring them in one bite and at the same time ordering his mother, with his mouth full: "Give us some more bubbly, maman, it's fairly decent," waving his knife in the air as though to help him attack the rabbit stew, whose aroma was making his broad, gluttonous nostrils quiver.

"Don't eat too well in Paris, eh son?"

"Oh, it isn't bad," Lucien grunted.

"There's going to be hail tomorrow," said a little girl whose hair was held at the top of her head by a pink ribbon, "and we won't be able to go to school."

After the sparkling wine came the ritual black coffee, very sweet, followed by a rosé wine, then a white wine from Nantes, and finally an apricot liqueur, "you can't say no, it's my mother's recipe, and the cassis too, it's my aunt Angéline's secret, she's the wife of my uncle Jean-Marie whose liver's being stewed in booze . . . We'll go and visit him tomorrow, and the *eau-de-vie,* no you'll never taste anything better than what we have here . . . in our hamlet!" After yielding to all his hosts' supplications, Mathieu Lelièvre felt that the fog which was already covering fields and valleys was entering the house, cloaking all the faces around the table in a moving, diaphanous jelly. He was about to hold out his hand to one of these forms when Lucien took him by the arm.

"Don't fall out of your chair. Come on, we'll grab a snooze in my corner, over there, in the pigsty . . . If you don't mind practically sleeping on the ground, I made the bed myself, and the bookcase too . . . I can see you aren't used to the local stuff . . . " Before Mathieu left the "big room," he saw the vast silhouette of Lucien's mother as she bent down to light the fire in the fireplace again; above it was a picture of Christ pointing with a long finger that had never known manual labour to his heart dripping bloody sweat. In the bed, Raphael was already asleep, his head turned to the wall, his abundant black curly hair covering the pillow, while three of his sisters formed a circle around him, sitting on the bed and turning the pages of *La Pharisienne* with a worried expression, a deep furrow crossing their foreheads.

"I'll turn the lights out soon," said the mother. "You forget that electricity's expensive. My legs can't hold me up any more."

"No, maman, not yet," said Solange. "We want to read Lucien's book. He brought it from Paris."

Mathieu Lelièvre staggered to Lucien's bed, bringing with him these fleeting scenes: the fire still sighing, the dogs, having eaten all the crumbs under the table, lying in untidy silence . . . Lucien picked up a little cat by the scruff of its neck and cooed against its belly: "My nasty tabby's growing up, he's already showing his claws . . . " and then the fog closed in on them once more. They had left the warmth of the house behind.

"Come on, let's go outside for a piss. Pépé's likely asleep in the loo and what good would it do us? The loo's outside; it's not like in Paris . . . My little room isn't bad, you'll see."

Mathieu slept happily, something he hadn't done for some time, but he remembered nothing except that long before he lay down, fully clothed, on his "pallet, no but it's a bed of torture . . . " Lucien had grumbled, Lucien had scrupulously read the local newspapers and only closed his eyes when he held forth on the *oeuvre* of Bataille, not saying as he had the night before, "not bad, not bad," but "my friend, it's fantastic. Ah, what an ass! Why bother bringing home someone I can talk to? That ass is already snoring!"

Lucien and Mathieu were awakened early next morning by a violent hailstorm and they saw, like a sudden squall, Mémé standing in the middle of the yard, among the hens, shooing away the shrill-voiced roosters and screaming like them herself, announcing as though it were good news: "Jean-Marie's going to pass on today for sure."

"No, no, Mémé, you told us that yesterday but he drank some bouillon."

"If not today, then tomorrow," said Mémé, irritated at her daugher's opposition. "I hope you'll come and pay the poor man a little visit. And I hear that Lucien's back from Paris. I heard the dogs barking last night and Pépé was tight the way he always is on Friday so he didn't hear a thing. Where's my grandson? I always said, we should keep him here in the fold because when they go to Paris they come back all changed . . . Listen, there's Pépé singing. He's taking the kid out to pasture . . . she still doesn't want anything to do with a billygoat and there's nothing we can do about it. Even though we brought in the liveliest one in the *canton,* the one with curly hair, there was nothing to be done about it. And where's your husband?"

"He had a calf to deliver. He didn't sleep. Don't stand there in the hail, Mémé, come inside where it's warm. I've got some strong coffee; if we don't drink it, it'll go to waste."

As Mathieu walked out of the pigsty with Lucien, he understood why the landscape he had only caught a glimpse of in the dark when they arrived, late, at the farm, looked like no other: a mysterious sorrow emanated from this isolated hamlet that was not illuminated by the light of day; night was never far away, like the ochre tones of the earth around the café where they had stopped on their way, and the vegetation was benign even in winter. One could admire the brightly coloured flashes in the extremely subtle sky that was veiled in the same dark greys and blues the peasants wore and seemed as sensitive to changing moods as they were. Against the oppressive and never-changing background that was the routine of these people, broad rose and orange shafts of light suddenly unleashed by the sky, even in the midst of hail or rain, fell upon the sombre stability of stone houses, orderly fields and valleys teeming with white flocks of sheep, but they did not lighten the sorrow that was the sorrow of the land itself and of those who were bowed down by it. Mathieu felt this desolation most of all as he looked at Lucien's mother, her legs puffy with varicose veins; it seemed that this woman alone, with her youthful and still pleasant body resting on those exhausted legs, represented all the silent drama of the women who had come before her and those who would follow.

"No little hailstorm's going to drive me indoors," said Mémé, still in a fighting spirit. But Lucien's mother, Mathieu thought, belonged to another race, a race of people born of the earth and living in harmony with it — but for how long? This small woman with the round bosom and eagle eyes, who wrapped her legs, those of a pert young girl, in ribbed black stockings, had sprung from the soil before his eyes, and she was as tenacious and proud as a hundred-year-old tree that has been touched by time only on its surface.

"It's sure; will you come and say a prayer for him?"

"Wait, Mémé, he's still alive," said Lucien's mother.

"And while you're there we can drink a bit of cassis," said Mémé. "Now where's that young rascal Lucien? Ah! there you are. Have you found yourself a woman in Paris? When's the wedding?"

"I don't know, Mémé, I don't know."

"Good-looking boy like you, sturdy too, you have to get married, that's all there is to it."

Then, masking her suspicion of "foreigners" (even those who came from a nearby village that she didn't know), Mémé cast her customary sly glace at Mathieu.

"Is that one of your friends from Paris?"

"No, Mémé, not from Paris. From America . . . "

"America, eh?" Mémé murmured dreamily.

"It's far away, very far," said Lucien.

"Oh yes, the poor thing, he comes from far away," said Méme, still dreamy.

Then, back bent, slender, her cold-reddened hand grasping her stick, Mémé followed her daughter into the house, saying in her shrill voice that was quarrelsome but gay: "If there's any strong coffee we can't let it go to waste."

Inside the house the fire had gone out and Raphael, whose fever had gone down during the night, woke up, and sitting in his bed, greeted the day with its fresh colour.

As he was returning to Paris, Mathieu Lelièvre gradually lost the intoxicating hopes of human landscapes that he brought back from his travels across the French countryside (even when he only hopped on a train to go to Chartres). When the train pulled into the station and he heard the brakes stopping and the usual mechanical rattle that signalled an arrival, and shortly before the whistle of the big engine that was still panting when the travellers jostled one another on the platforms, he felt then that by leaving the countryside or the sea behind him he would find "her" again – Madame d'Argenti, spread out like the winter fog, the fog that was at times so tenacious, "over all of Paris," for most of all he feared meeting her outside, leaving a tea room at five o'clock or going to her coiffeur at that hour when the light abounds, pitilessly, on all forms of lassitude and, at the same time, the church bells of Paris remind workers that their garlic sausage sandwich or their cassoulet or choucroute is waiting for them in cafés or corner bistros. Mathieu knew that Madame d'Argenti would never deign to set foot in such shelters. Late at night or very early in the morning, when he was walking through deserted stations or crossing empty boulevards – like a series of funeral sites – he felt the "sensation of Yvonne d'Argenti's sleep" rise up in him with the cold of his homecoming; for was she not sleeping now beside the innocent Peter, who was heedless of the slow moral destruction awaiting him? Peter, beneath the watchful eye of Victor the cat, a creature so conniving, Mathieu thought, that he finally resembled Madame d'Argenti; a member of her fateful entourage, had he not renounced the life of a cat in order to be a woman so he could lie as well as his mistress? To avoid meeting Yvonne d'Argenti at his door, Mathieu had

148

got in the habit of going home only to sleep; as for the letter from Pierre-Henri Lajeunesse he expected any day, he gradually became resigned to never receiving it. He would do more writing in the cafés, and eat less; that way he would get through the winter. Ah! he thought, if only Madame d'Argenti hadn't eaten away part of his body and his soul, but no. Her ogress's whims had robbed him of "the two finest seasons in Paris, spring and summer." Despite her spectre, which sometimes went so far as to assume the shape of a cloud or the taste of peaches because they had eaten them together in Tunis, Mathieu marvelled at his freedom, as escaped prisoners do. One evening when he was roaming through the Paris evening he was so fond of, he had a surprise that would become for him the obverse side of his happiness: the joy of a Québécois in Paris. For life must be a poem if it leads you first to the d'Argentis' house, their cosy hell, and then a few months later to a discreet street, to the sign of a café inviting you to let time slip away at "Les Heures Enfuies." Was it not in Paris that you encountered, for your sins, a character from Balzac in your bed and, to reward you, a fragment of Things Past in a modern café with some musty atmosphere still snuggling in its lair? And yet, at Les Heures Enfuies, the brightness of the past was turning yellow too: Mathieu had scarcely entered an ancient tiny room, its walls covered with red velvet reminiscent of the d'Argentis' vestibule (which was adorned with the same coat rack, the same gilded frame around the mirror and the same old-fashioned telephone) when Monsieur Paul, the proprietor, walked ceremoniously towards him to warn him that "this side of the banquette is torn . . . Yes, we must repair it, look at the leather, worn out by the years . . . but repair means destruction and here, it's the character of things that matters . . . Look, if you're going to write you'll be more comfortable here . . . Ah yes! many poets used to come here . . . but it's quite different now." In a short time Mathieu became an habitué of the bar. He no longer left his table, his books and his notebooks, and the table, a precise copy of a schoolboy's desk with its heavy iron feet, had been offered to him quite spontaneously by Monsieur Paul as soon as he saw Mathieu standing on the purple rug whose corners curled back like flower petals. "Some shade, Jean-Loup, if you please," he implored. He was tall, with the head of an academician who loved life, for if his forehead was that of a wise man, his cheeks seemed radiant from wine and mountain air. And as soon as Monsieur Paul saw "the writer" as he called him respectfully, Mathieu was so touched that when he opened his notebooks on the desk he took a long look around him but lacked the courage to write a single word.

"I knew all the cafés and all the bars in Paris in my day; if you only knew all we do about life . . . My friends are dead . . . The poets too . . . Ah! my young friend, if you'd known my café as it once was! Everything's changed, but in those days we had a role in the lives of our artists and writers . . . But today, who needs me?"

"We need you, Monsieur Paul," murmured Madame Lola at the bar, her nose in her wine punch.

"Ah! you say that because you're an artist, Madame Lol, a pianist."

"Pianist: well, I was once but with this punch I get punchy Monsieur Paul, and now I only run on red, as they say."

The fauna that swarmed endlessly at the bar (which was raised like an altar and similarly marked by rituals and processions) while lower down Mathieu wrote – in the small room near the altar, which allowed the various brotherhoods to join together their various forms of intimacy without disturbing them – exerted a fascination over his imagination that, like a drug, he could no longer do without. He thought of everything that might have escaped his images of France if he had never met Monsieur Paul and heard him speak of long-gone writers, or Madame Lola who was like a small girl made prematurely old by the exhaustion of alcohol and the fever of a nomadic existence; Madame Lola who, when she danced to fire up her intoxication and that of her friends was as fragile and almost as transparent in her wild and spindly leaps as a dragonfly. "You know, you'd never guess to see me like this, but I'm a proper woman, very good looking. I used to be in novels; everyone in Paris used to talk about me. They know me everywhere – in the bars and all the hospitals too. A little cure does you good sometimes . . . And then your stomach starts to dissolve, you know what I mean? But we artists must be fed too. The State has a duty. Lots of young people have stripped my apartment bare. I used to be rich, but now I have nothing. Do you like these navy trousers I bought at La Baule? No, Mireille gave them to me, the dear child is always giving me presents. She's not like the young people who come to my apartment and take off with my belongings . . . I used to trust them, they were communists, but you should never trust anyone. Hasn't Alphonse come to play the piano to-night? Sleeping in the Métro again, I suppose. Ah! The ravages of wine! Jean-Loup, where's Mireille, your sweet little wife?"

"She'll be here soon, Madame Lol, she's late because of the child."

"Again? All right, but Mireille's my angel. I tell everyone. Only yesterday she made me eat soup and dumplings. 'Ah! On the smooth-skinned snow.' Do you know that song? Another little drink, Jean-Loup?"

"It would be nicer to wait for Mireille. She likes to buy it for you when you're on your fifth, Madame Lol."

"What? This is only the third, Jean-Loup."

"It's the sixth, Madame Lol," Jean-Loup replied with masterful poise.

This young man who served customers calmly and aristocratically, for in this bar if he was asked for a "planter's punch" by someone wearing a doctor's white smock (or on other evenings, a student's blue one) he would abandon the hectic agitation of the drinkers standing or sometimes hunched over the "zinc" that looked its fifty years ("no rest for the bartender in this business. Ah! it's not the way it was when Mireille and I were in New York . . . there they respect our métier; and in Africa, when people are well-off there, respect, you understand what I'm saying Monsieur, they know how to respect other people in those countries!") the better to concentrate on decanting the pink alcohol whose secret he possessed: he did not serve a punch but, in keeping with a tradition worthy of an alchemist, the pinkish concoction he poured into the flute glasses seemed to have been prepared by his mind as much as by his precise actions. The flight of night birds drinking, exchanging insults or lulling one another with tender words that were quickly dashed with gall on "the altar" of the bar, rarely brought him a reprimand or even an intolerant look. His profession went beyond any rudeness and, like God, he knew men without having to look at them. He heard them. "Hi, little lamb," a black-haired girl said to her "guy." "Hi, fats," he replied. "That's not my name, Totor." "I'll call you whatever I please, but you're my queen. Oh yes, you're my baby and I love you!" Totor replied. "Were you with Fifi again?" "You're slipping, pussycat." Jean-Loup could predict the conversations between Totor and his friend depending on the day and time – again, like God the Father, he had nothing to learn from the good and evil deeds that fell onto his scale; he predicted them as he distilled the pure and the impure in his cocktails; like a healer, he was an expert in using benign poisons to soothe human pain.

"Come on, Jean-Loup, do something. This old pig on my left wants to rape me."

"Aren't you exaggerating a little, Céline?"

"My ass is my property and this guy, the corporal, what's your name? this lecher who used to be in the army, no, now stop that, there, you see? he's pawing me; now I'm not saying I don't like doing it in the proper time and place, but tonight's the wrong night; I lost my man yesterday. What do men think about, Jean-Loup? Fucking! And it's disgusting. Look at your corporal, jerking off behind my back! What a dirty old man!"

"Everyone is respected here; yes, everyone," said Jean-Loup. "We all have our bad habits."

"As the song says," said Madame Lola, " 'I was a virgin –
but when?' Ah! Here's Alphonse. Let's open the old piano
. . . He's going to play . . . He won a second prize at the conservatory, like me . . . Alphonse, dear friend, let me introduce a writer who hails from those snowy lands of which
you and I know nothing . . . let's go now, my friend, there's
no heat in my apartment, I'll catch my death . . . Let's go
visit this boy . . . He's nice and he looks like a good sort. He
offered me a second drink . . . How did the song go, Alphonse? Play it for me . . . 'The snow . . . the spray . . . the six
waves carry us along.' " Alphonse spoke little, a few words
about the war sometimes, and of an obscure, distant time
"when I was a millionaire," he said, and as for "the second
prize at the conservatory" he spoke of it only with sad regret. All of Alphonse's person, forever regretting and heavy
with sighs, seemed encrusted in the décor of Les Heures Enfuies. His creased skin beneath grey hair shared with the
leather of the easy chairs the same melancholy wrinkles, the
same cracks as well, and his tired voice matched the blues
on the record player, while the plaid coat, shiny with wear,
which he hung in the vestibule was one of those objects that
in the lives of unhappy men speak for them, seeming to be
carved forever in the memories of places.

"Fall asleep in the Métro again, my dear Alphonse?" Madame Lola asked, suddenly quite vigorous even though she
had just announced to everyone that "the night before she'd
had more than in six months . . . what's the use of living
when people think only of stealing your possessions, even
your sheets, eh? No, the State should pay for funerals."

"Yes," Alphonse replied lugubriously.

"The grilles in the Métro are warmer nowadays," said
Madame Lola. "That's good. So, we'll play a little Chopin to
loosen up our fingers . . . On your feet. Alphonse, and hold
me . . . I'm going to fall . . . if my bones started getting soft,
oh la la! Really, it would be a disaster! What's important is
to be happy, what do you say about that? Don't I know
every hostel in Paris? And all the hospitals too? For a woman
from a good family, it's honest . . . "

"You're irreplaceable," said Alphonse gloomily. They got up, Alphonse with an ancient pair of tennis shoes hanging from a string around his neck and his chin badly shaven: "You have to carry your house on your back when you sleep outside," he said. Through the grace of a playful camaraderie they both found only at the piano, Alphonse and Madame Lola, who smiled so seldom, suddenly in the confusion of their bizarre symphonies they began to play, laugh, and talk at the same time.

"All the hostels, Madame Lola? Even the one at Bordeaux?"

"No, but I've been in the ones in Provence and Angoulême. They knew who you were in those places . . . Ah! that was bohemian life . . . and the knowledge of abjection, alas! comes only from the abject . . .

"That's true indeed, true indeed."

At nine o'clock, Jean-Loup looked up from his concoctions to greet with a tender look the woman everyone was waiting for at that hour, even though they had to wait a long time "because that young scamp of a Jean-Loup who's so different from his father and doesn't stand still for a moment; well, I had to stick him in the bathtub with all his clothes on, he was so covered with mud . . . " Mireille had come directly from her native Pyrenees into this purgatory steaming with every human sin, which she understood as well as her husband, even though she demanded more retribution than he when she spoke, talking of the "riffraff" she was nonetheless quite fond of, forgiving one person's vices, another's "strange little ways," in the name of "human baseness – on which I could give you an entire dossier, my friend, believe me!" but demanding of everyone "dignity, yes, and most of all, that people don't assume they have the right to touch me . . . No, that's something I won't tolerate." Her bewitching accent, her always inspired and descriptive way of speaking as well as her supreme youth and beauty made her invaluable and venerable to all. An evening "without Mireille," as Madame Lola said, was "an evening without punch . . . "

"You look lovely tonight, darling."

"I have a friend in the fashion business, he's so kind . . . Ah! I haven't forgotten your winter shoes, Madame Lola, it's time to replace your clogs and I have them with me."

"Darling, I love you. Without you it would be night, it's always night except when you're here. No dumplings though, I have a stomach ache."

"But you must eat something, Madame Lol," Mireille replied.

"The bird doesn't live off its song? Ah, darling, you look so adorable in your orange dress. I love it. Alphonse, this child gives me an appetite for life . . . Do you love me, darling? If you do, why should I die, my angel? In any case, I'll have some bread and butter . . . and a bit of cheese too . . . Yes, Alphonse do you remember the song: 'They launched an attack on my nipples at Grenelle . . . ' "

"I'll get it ready right away, Madame Lol, and I'll bring you your punch. And your beer, Alphonse." Mathieu Lelièvre seemed unaware that although at nine o'clock he had, like Jean-Loup silently welcoming his wife, looked up from his *oeuvre*, it was because he too, like the others, was delighted when Mireille appeared in the bar. As he drank Jean-Loup's delicious cocktails, at the same time savouring the highly cultivated Monsieur Paul, he felt a pang of joy when Mireille, interrupting her activities, came and sat across from him and had a drink at his table. He felt then that Madame d'Argenti had always treated him only as an "absence," never addressing his entire being but rather some part of his person that she might use; it was only now, as Mireille watched him, that he became "a presence," a complete person.

"Did your work go well today, Mathieu? Writing a book must be very hard; I couldn't do it, though I know so much about people. In a bar you can explore all the possibilities of society so quickly. Oh, there are scenes I could describe to you . . . The people in this bar are all quite different, and really quite lovely . . . but it's not that way everywhere . . .

155

Ah! you know, I don't always like the French . . . Sometimes they're so bigoted, narrow-minded. Perhaps it's because they don't travel enough . . . When my husband and I were in Africa, the people we were ashamed of were quite often our own people . . . In America too . . . I'm talking about the French of Paris in particular! But I'll let you work . . . Madame Lol's waiting for her bread and cheese."

"I like young girls and I like young women even more," Madame Lola crooned at the piano.

"Poor Madame Lol, she must be famished. She hasn't eaten for three days and she really likes her wine . . . Will you come and see us tomorrow night? We'd like to have you join us."

How could Mathieu resist these invitations? (He sometimes lingered in the bar until closing time, when Jean-Loup pulled the black grille over the grey letters of "Les Heures Enfuies".) He was accustomed to these conversations with Mireille, even when she told him of "the child's dangerous antics . . . No, young Jean-Loup is a clever one, if you only knew . . . I'll send him to his grandparents soon, for a rest, in the Pyrenees . . . On Sundays when he and his father go off on their bicycles I get some peace . . . I adore the child, he's full of life . . . a little too much like me and not enough like his father . . . " Mathieu liked the warm colour of her eyes, the expression of a rugged will on her pure features, absolutely free of guile. Like him she was "an individual" and she knew how to listen with an attentiveness he thought he did not deserve, especially when he told her of problems that were quite foreign to her. "Ah! I can imagine . . . yes, how patient I would have to be to write one chapter after the other . . . I can't even finish a letter to my mother," she would reply, her cheek resting on her fist, her short hair scarcely covering the top of her forehead and her ears. After a few evenings at Les Heures Enfuies he thought Mireille might be that person he had so hoped to find in Paris: a friend. And that was how Mathieu finally broke away from the memory of Madame d'Argenti. One morning when he got up she was no longer there, not in his thoughts or in his fears. Madame d'Argenti had disappeared into the shadows, "deaf to any appeal for pity" as she had written of one of the heroines in her novels.

He did not see her again. Spring was coming and Mathieu Lelièvre had to think of leaving Paris, and with the city, all the people in it who were dear to him. He went from one café to another, saying goodbye "but only for a while" – to a Corsican friend in his café on rue d'Assas, to his stalwart Norman friend, to two brothers in their bar in Saint-Germain who were, like Monsieur Paul, pillars of a distant, vanished time, to the Papa and Mama in their café on rue de Vaugirard – the Papa had recited Dante to him while the Mama praised her country, Sicily. And how many others had he forgotten, he wondered, as he travelled across Paris – all those noble people, their nobility not the sort made up of privilege and arrogance like that of Yvonne d'Argenti, but rather of the quality of their feelings, of an innate probity that not everyone is privileged to possess . . . By chance, he saw Antoine d'Argenti and Ashmed. Antoine was looking for Ashmed, who had just run away with some dubious friends from the Quartier Latin and Antoine was trying unsuccessfully to "bring him back home." Ashmed had grown and he took Mathieu's hand in his own small, dry one.

"Come with us, we're going to eat couscous . . . Some of my pals invited us to their restaurant."

"Yes, do come Mathieu, it would be so pleasant!" said Antoine d'Argenti, who seemed exhausted. His narrow head was buried in a winter hat of Venetian elegance. Yes, Mathieu thought, it would be pleasant, "because the child is so fond of you." Mathieu accepted because he too was "fond" of Ashmed and Antoine. However, "because of that woman" he knew that Antoine already sensed what he had experienced many times: that it was the end of a friendship . . . That eating couscous together was only "one last favour, out of love for Ashmed."

"With sauce, Ali, my father's hungry and so am I . . . Will you come and play at the shooting gallery with me, at the café on rue de Buci, Mathieu?"

"No, not this time" Mathieu replied.

"Mohammed, give us some bread. Will you come and play with me then, Mohammed?" Ashmed asked, bouncing so much with delight that Antoine couldn't make him sit still.

"Come now, calm down a bit," said Antoine d'Argenti ir-ritably. "I've had a hard day at the Bank. Everything's going very badly today," he said to Mathieu suddenly. "I must find work for the child . . . perhaps here, in this restaurant, who knows . . . he could do the cleaning . . . I'm dreadfully in debt because of my children . . . and Yvonne can become so violent" (he murmured this last word in a low voice for fear of Ashmed's indiscretion) "if I keep him at home . . . Since he's afraid of her he keeps running away . . . his friends . . . unfortunately a bunch of delinquents . . . thieves . . . what can I do?" he lamented with a grimace of pain, "what can I do? My friend, I wanted so much to help this child . . . But if it fails will it be because of her? Or because of me?"

"Because of her," said Mathieu, who was awakening from the lethargy he had experienced in the company of Yvonne d'Argenti. "Before I knew Yvonne," he went on, "I didn't believe in the existence of responsible monsters, of deliber-ate criminals . . . but everything's changed . . . for me . . . yes, everything."

"They are only sick people, and we should take pity on them," said Antoine d'Argenti angrily. "Now let's change the subject, I beg you."

Soon they left, and never saw one another again. Ashmed, who didn't understand and who had yielded to his friends' fickle charm during the meal, laughed heartily, showing his friends "Ashmed's beard," a fine down above his pink lips. He seized Mathieu's hand and implored him to "come and play with Ashmed now and then, he's bored . . . Yes, my fa-ther's often angry now; sometimes I think he doesn't love his little boy any more."

"Now, now, you're trying to seduce us with your words, Ashmed," said Antoine d'Argenti in the same irritated tone. "Come now, let's go home."

"And Paul?" Mathieu asked, suddenly remembering this existence which seemed that of a wounded man or a convalescent.

"Paul? He's going to be cabin boy on a boat. As Etienne says, it's all he knows how to do, alas! Fortunately he likes the sea."

They walked away. Antoine's slender silhouette seemed to be carried on the wind as he held onto his broad chestnut-colored velvet hat with one hand with the other drew Ashmed towards him; but the child kept turning around and calling out to Mathieu: "Say you'll come and play with Ashmed. Will you?" Antoine went on walking quickly, not turning around.

A few hours before his departure, Mathier Lelièvre was polishing his boots when he received the letter he had given up expecting. The envelope from Pierre-Henri Lajeunesse telling him it was "for laughs" that he had been sent "to Yvonne d'Argenti; yes, to see how the hare would make out in this trial . . . very badly, I see . . . Ah! but that's because your servile heart went along with the game . . . I did too. After all, I already knew about Madame d'Argenti's fashionable weaknesses, but now I've renounced all that. And do you know why? Because you who knew me when I sported a cane and kid gloves, and gold in my pockets to please the women for whom one must buy things – like your friend, our Madame d'Argenti – you'll see me tomorrow, comrade, stripped of everything. Very little hair (I've cut it all off) and not only a revolutionary and ready to take up arms but . . . " Pierre-Henri went on to explain that "before giving away all his money" he had been "unable to come to the help of a friend . . . but it's time for you to return to your country, traitor that you are." Another letter, this one from Lucien, announced to Mathieu "the death of Uncle Jean-Marie whom you visited, remember? He died peacefully in the

159

white room you saw with Mémé and me. Poor Mémé, she was fidgeting on her chair as she said her rosary, still dreaming of her cassis. After the funeral we killed a hen at the farm; pity you weren't there, we'll probably not see each other again because America is too far away for us and our parents are poor. But if you ever want to see the Côte Sauvage again – no, what filth life is. I wanted to tell you that Uncle Jean-Marie moaned a few times, in his delirium, 'They're killing the pig, eh? They're killing the pig.' He wasn't conscious, but he could sense it. Well, that's all the news from our hamlet, I think. Au revoir. Lucien."

And so his journey was over; an inner journey that was as perilous as it was overwhelming with unexpected discoveries. Shortly before the airplane took off, Mathieu called Mireille just to hear her voice, and that voice had the power to bury the other one, the first one, the one that had moved him with its feigned hesitations, its calculated sighs – the voice he would never hear again.

"We'll miss you at Les Heures Enfuies," said Mireille.

"What's good is that France isn't very far from us," said Mathieu.

"That's true; in fact it's really quite close, like the Pyrenees."

Mathieu left that night, flying back home, thinking he had lived "a story, like one in a book." And now he had closed that troubling book. In a way, Madame d'Argenti was dead. He could make her live again only through literature, and once again he would be told that "novels aren't the same as life."